Twayne's United States Authors Series

EDITOR OF THIS VOLUME

David Nordloh

Indiana University

Thomas Wentworth Higginson

TUSAS 313

Thomas Wentworth Higginson

THOMAS WENTWORTH HIGGINSON

By JAMES W. TUTTLETON

New York University

TWAYNE PUBLISHERS

A DIVISION OF G. K. HALL & CO., BOSTON

Published in 1978 by Twayne Publishers,
A Division of G. K. Hall & Co.
All Rights Reserved

Printed on permanent / durable acid-free paper and bound
in the United States of America

First Printing

Library of Congress Cataloging in Publication Data

Tuttleton, James W
  Thomas Wentworth Higginson.

  (Twayne's United States authors series; 313)
  Bibliography: p. 163 - 166
  Includes index.
  1. .Higginson, Thomas Wentworth, 1823 - 1911—Criticism and
interpretation.
PS1928.T88   818'.4'09   78-3472
ISBN 0-8057-7236-7

Contents

About the Author

Preface

Chronology

1. The Life of Thomas Wentworth Higginson   13

2. First Principles of a Man of Letters   51

3. The Emancipation of Blacks: *Army Life in a Black Regiment* 59

4. The Liberation of Half of the Human Race: *Common
   Sense About Women*   74

5. The Craft of Expression: Higginson as a Romancer, Poet,
   and Public Speaker   82

6. The Craft of Herodotus: Higginson as an Historian   102

7. The Craft of Plutarch: Higginson as a Biographer   111

8. The Craft of Criticism: Higginson on American Writing   126

9. Epilogue: Higginson and the Equation of Fame   148

   Notes and References   153

   Selected Bibliography   163

   Index   167

About the Author

James W. Tuttleton is Chairman of the Department of English at New York University. A graduate of Harding College, he received the M.A. and Ph.D. degrees from the University of North Carolina at Chapel Hill. He formerly taught at Clemson University, the University of North Carolina and the University of Wisconsin. His field of specialization is American literature of the nineteenth and twentieth centuries.

A member of the Modern Language Association, the American Studies Association, and the Century Association, Mr. Tuttleton is the author of a number of articles on American writing, as well as *The Novel of Manners in America* and two forthcoming studies, *Edith Wharton: The Critical Heritage* and *Henry James's The American: A Critical Edition*. He is also the editor of Washington Irving's *Voyages and Discoveries of the Companions of Columbus*, which will be published by Twayne Publishers.

Preface

Although Thomas Wentworth Higginson was a minor radical activist and man of letters, he had what Henry James called "the interesting quality of having reflected almost everything that was in the New England air"[1] during his time (1823 - 1911). A student at Harvard College in the late 1830s, he was liberated by the currents of Emersonian Transcendentalism which swept through the school. And as a Divinity School student and ordained minister, he broke with the doctrines of rational Unitarianism and embraced a religion of natural feeling and Christian love, which he put to the service of a fiery abolitionism. Along with Wendell Phillips, Theodore Parker, and others, the Reverend Mr. Higginson astounded Boston by leading a citizens' assault on the Court House in 1854 to free Anthony Burns, a fugitive slave being held there. Increasingly hostile to the "peculiar institution" of slavery in the late 1850s, he procured arms for the antislavery emigrants to Kansas and, as one of the revolutionary "Secret Six," conspired with John Brown to smuggle escaped slaves into Canada. The high point of his career as a radical was his appointment, during the Civil War, to the command of the first regiment of ex-slaves in the Union army. He led the invasion and occupation of Jacksonville in 1863, was wounded leading his black troops in South Carolina, and was discharged a hero in 1864. I have tried to tell the exciting story of his life in chapter one of the present study, for the dramatic paradoxes of his career illuminate the antebellum and Civil War years in an especially vivid way.

But Colonel Higginson was more than a militant abolitionist and Union soldier. He was also a representative man of letters in Boston during the latter half of the nineteenth century. The study of his writing offers, therefore, a mirror of the literature of his age—which spanned the "Flowering of New England," as Van Wyck Brooks put it, and "New England's Indian Summer."

Extraordinarily popular as a familiar essayist for the *Atlantic Monthly*, Higginson published scores of books and articles on the arts and letters in England and America, on nature and physical culture, on liberal reform in racial relations and woman's suffrage, on civil service and the school system, and on temperance, evolutionary science, New England history, and politics. In the present volume, I have tried to offer a comprehensive view of the written work of a Brahmin of extraordinary literary range and catholic taste.

After the opening biographical portrait, chapter two defines the first principles of his social and literary criticism, which were based on the doctrines of liberal Christianity and social democracy. Chapter three explores the application of those principles to the racial situation, culminating in a discussion of that neglected masterpiece *Army Life in a Black Regiment.* The fourth chapter traces his crusade in behalf of women's liberation, waged on the platform at many feminist conventions and articulated persuasively in *Common Sense About Women.* As he aspired to be an artist, chapter five explores his imaginative expression in *Malbone: A Romance* and in his poems, stories, oratory, and translations. Less belletristic is the body of writing analyzed in chapters six and seven, his historical prose and his biographical studies—the latter principally of literary figures like Longfellow, Whittier, and Margaret Fuller, all of whom he intimately knew. Chapter eight examines his genteel literary criticism, as illustrated in scores of studies of the major American writers of his time. Finally, chapter nine, the epilogue, addresses itself to the strengths and weaknesses of Thomas Wentworth Higginson, as man and writer, in relation to the question of "the equation of fame," which he called the first business of criticism.

Throughout, my aim in this book has been to give a comprehensive overview of the man and his work, so as to make his contribution to American life and letters more widely known than it now is. But aside from illuminating his exciting age, the works of Higginson have a considerable intrinsic merit—an admirable intellectual range, a generousness of spirit, and a gratifying charm of style. I have therefore also tried to suggest to the interested reader the considerable basis for a greater appreciation of his mind and his work.

JAMES W. TUTTLETON

New York University

Chronology

1823   Thomas Wentworth Higginson born on December 23 in Cambridge, Mass., the tenth and last child of Louisa (Storrow) and Stephen Higginson, Jr.

1837   Admitted to Harvard College, age 13.

1841   Graduated from Harvard; became a tutor.

1844   Entered the Harvard Divinity School. Graduated in 1847, a disciple of the Transcendental "Newness."

1847   Married to Mary Channing, the niece of William Ellery Channing; called to the Unitarian pulpit of the First Religious Society of Newburyport, Mass.; became an active abolitionist and Free Soil party nominee for Congress.

1849   Resigned his pulpit; lectured on nature, antislavery.

1850   Nominated for Congress in the 3rd District by the Free Soil party; defeated, he counseled disobedience to the Fugitive Slave Law; advocated liberal labor laws, election reforms, founded a free school for mill workers.

1851   Led the Boston Vigilance Committee in a vain attempt to rescue the escaped slave Thomas Sims.

1852   Accepted the Free Church pulpit in Worcester, Mass.

1853   Addressed the Massachusetts Anti-Slavery Society and the Whole World's Temperance Convention with Garrison, Phillips, Susan B. Anthony, Lucy Stone and others; edited (with Samuel Longfellow) *Thalatta* (sea poems).

1854   Fugitive slave Anthony Burns arrested in Boston. Higginson procured handaxes, led the mob on the Court House; the attempt failed, a policeman was killed; Higginson, wounded, was indicted but never tried.

1856   Formed the Massachusetts-Kansas Aid Committee to assist Free Soil emigrants; bought arms, traveled with them to Kansas.

1857   Resigned pulpit; assembled the State Disunion Convention in Worcester; advocated revolution and the dissolution of the Union.

1858   Conspired with the "Secret Six" to aid John Brown.

1859   John Brown's raid on Harper's Ferry fails; Higginson not indicted.

1862   Colonel Higginson appointed to command of the First S.C. Volunteers, the first regiment of freed slaves in the Union army; began correspondence with Emily Dickinson.

1863   Directed the invasion and occupation of Jacksonville; wounded in an engagement near Beaufort, S.C.

1864   Discharged with a medical disability; settled in Newport.

1865   Translated *Works of Epictetus;* advocated reconstruction.

1866   Edited *Harvard Memorial Biographies.*

1869   *Malbone: An Oldport Romance* (fiction).

1870   *Army Life in a Black Regiment;* helped to found the American Woman Suffrage Association and *Woman's Journal* (coeditor, 1870 - 1884). Met Emily Dickinson in Amherst.

1871   *Atlantic Essays.*

1873   *Oldport Days.*

1875   *Young Folks' History of the United States.*

1877   Mary died on September 2; *A Book of American Explorers.*

1879   Returned to Cambridge; married Mary Thacher.

1880   Elected to the Massachusetts State Legislature (for two years). *Short Studies of American Authors.*

1881   Daughter Margaret Waldo born. *Common Sense About Women.*

1884   *Margaret Fuller Ossoli* (biography).

1885   *A Larger History of the United States.*

1887   *Hints on Writing and Speech-making.*

1889   Lectured at the Lowell Institute; *Travellers and Outlaws.*

1890   Edited with Mabel Loomis Todd *Poems by Emily Dickinson; Life and Times of Francis Higginson.*

1891   Edited with Mabel Loomis Todd *Poems by Emily Dickinson: Second Series.*

1892   *Concerning All of Us; The New World and the New Book.*

1893   *Such As They Are: Poems* (with Mary T. Higginson); *English History for American Readers* (with Edward Channing).

1895   *Massachusetts in the Army and Navy during the Civil War.*

1896   *Cheerful Yesterdays* (autobiography).

1897   *Book and Heart: Essays on Literature and Life.*

1899   *Contemporaries.*

1900   *Writings of Thomas Wentworth Higginson* (7 vols.).

1902   *Henry Wadsworth Longfellow* (biography); *John Greenleaf Whittier* (biography).
1903   *Reader's History of American Literature* (with H. W. Boynton).
1905   *Part of a Man's Life.*
1907   *Life and Times of Stephen Higginson.*
1909   *Carlyle's Laugh, and Other Surprises.*
1911   *Descendants of the Reverend Francis Higginson;* died at 87 on May 9; buried at Mt. Auburn Cemetery in Cambridge.

CHAPTER 1

The Life of Thomas Wentworth Higginson

THOMAS Wentworth Higginson was born on December 22, 1823, in his father's house on "Professors' Row" in Cambridge, Massachusetts, the tenth and last child of Stephen Higginson, Jr., and Louisa Storrow Higginson. The Higginsons were of old New England stock, tracing their American descent from the Reverend Mr. Francis Higginson, who sailed in charge of the first large party of emigrants to the Massachusetts Bay Colony, landing at Salem in 1629.

On his mother's side, Thomas Wentworth Higginson was descended from the Appletons and Wentworths of New Hampshire, who boasted a royal governor in the family genealogy. His mother was born to an English officer in St. Andrews, Scotland, in 1786. His father, as bursar of Harvard College, planted the great elms in the Yard, directed the Harvard Divinity School, and enjoyed great wealth, until Jefferson's embargo ruined the shipping trade and the family fortune declined. He died when young Wentworth was ten, and the Higginson children were raised by their mother and her sister, "Aunt Nancy" Storrow. Partly because he was a sickly baby, kept alive, it was said, by the juice of chicken bones, and partly because he was reared in a household of women, young Wentworth was encouraged to pursue the athletic and manly life. And, later on, he never avoided an opportunity to test his physical and spiritual courage.

The character of the young boy, as well as his mother's special affection for him, may perhaps be inferred from her description of him when he was nine: "He has genuine refinement and delicacy, with manliness and power of controlling himself and a sense of right, governing his thoughts and actions—which command my *respect* as much as if he was a grown man. . . . I never [saw] one who was more thoughtful and considerate of others—though he has been the youngest and an object of uncommon interest."[1] His special affection for her was expressed many years later in an essay called "The Woman Who Most Influenced Me," where he observed: "In all the vicissitudes of a reformer's career, I cannot recall anything but encouragement on her part." He traced to her direct influence the "three leading motives of her youngest son's life—the love of personal liberty, of religious freedom, and of the equality of the sexes."[2]

I *Early Life In Cambridge*

Old Cambridge, in Higginson's youth, was a village of only two or three thousand people, and the boy in his ramblings came to know every inch of it. He was educated at the school of William Wells, "an Englishman of the old stamp, erect, vigorous, manly, who abhorred a mean or cowardly boy as he did a false quantity."[3] Young Wentworth was an apt scholar and suffered few of the customary cane whippings, but for his classmates Richard Henry Dana and C. C. Perkins, Wells's discipline was cruel and traumatic. Nevertheless, the Wells school, perhaps next to the Boston Latin School, offered the best preparation in Cambridge for a university education. And, at the age of thirteen, in 1837, Wentworth entered Harvard College, the youngest member of his class.

He was later to call himself "a child of the College,"[4] as indeed he was. But young Higginson's pastimes *outside* the classroom also had an important bearing on the boy's education. He loved nature, took long walks through the fields and woods, and developed a naturalist's knowledge of the New England countryside. He was a tall, strong, athletic boy—nearly six feet tall by the age of fourteen. He swam the Charles River at midnight and loved skating and playing ice hockey on the Fresh Pond, and played baseball, football, cricket, and tenpins on the green near Porter's Tavern.

Living in Cambridge in the 1830s was itself a preparation for the literary life he eventually embraced. For to the Higginson household came such luminaries as Henry Wadsworth Longfellow, Margaret Fuller, George Ticknor, and even (once) Washington Irving. Wentworth's nurse, Rowena Pratt, was the wife of Longfellow's "village blacksmith," and the boy regularly played in Oliver Wendell Holmes's library with the Autocrat's nephew, Charles Parsons. The Higginson library was the center of the household, and

Wentworth steeped his imagination in the novels of Scott, the British essayists, the works of Tasso and Ariosto, Spenser's *The Faerie Queene*, the majestic prose of Dr. Johnson, Boswell's *Life*, the novels of Fanny Burney and Maria Edgeworth, and the *Select British Poets*, which included Collins, Goldsmith, Byron, and Campbell. His reading habits, as well as his lifelong interest in the treatment of blacks, are suggested by a letter to his brother in Maryland, written when he was eleven: "I have got 5 more Waverley Novels since you have been gone: Ivanhoe, The Monastery, The Pirates, and the 1st and 2nd Series of Chronicles of the Canongate, besides Peveril of the Peak which you left behind. Sunday School is in the Courthouse now. . . . I shall like to hear about a fox-hunt. Are there any slaves at Mr. Martin's, and do they blow a conch in the morning to collect them? . . . I read the Spectator a few days ago."[5] Higginson learned his history from the writings of Bancroft and John Marshall and from Jared Sparks's American biographies. He read about birds, animals, and flowers, and was absorbed by the romantic adventures of "Baron Trenck," "Rinaldo Rinaldini," "The Three Spaniards," and "The Devil on Two Sticks." These romantic works excited his imagination and cultivated that passion for adventure which later found expression in his antislavery struggles and in combat during the Civil War. He also made an early discovery of Keats, Tennyson, and Browning, whom he avidly read with his childhood friends Jimmy (James Russell) Lowell and William Wetmore Story.

II *A Child of the College*

At Harvard, as a member of the class of 1841, Wentworth Higginson knew every one of its 305 students, all of its professors, including President Josiah Quincy, and every corner of the seven or eight buildings constituting the college. Classical languages formed a major part of his curriculum, and he mastered several modern languages, mathematics, history, and philosophy. Longfellow tutored him in French, Jones Very in Greek; Sparks taught the boy history; Benjamin Peirce and Nathaniel Bowditch taught him mathematics and calculus; and Edward Tyrell Channing, Boyleston Professor of Rhetoric and Oratory, taught him composition and forensics. Channing especially was a great teacher who shaped the prose style of many of the distinguished authors of the "New England Renaissance."[6] Thanks to his instruction, Higginson's later periodical essays perfected the familiar style in nineteenth-century America and—collected as *Atlantic Essays* (1871)—were assigned in schoolrooms across the country.

When Higginson entered Harvard, he was given an Abstract of Laws and Regulations governing attendance and dress. One rule read: "Dress. On Sabbaths and Exhibition days, and on all public occasions, each student in public shall wear a black or black-mixed coat, with buttons of the same color."[7] Higginson wore the prescribed uniform but—befitting the future radical—he was a troublesome student, probably because he was the youngest boy in the college and had few close friends. One of his college diaries notes: "The Prex sent for me. . . . He found I'd cut 17 prayers. . . . I must look out. Rather a bore, for I shall have to cut some more for skating." He went to Fowler, the phrenologist, who told him that he had "splendid talents" but no application, and Wentworth noted: "Lovering [one of his tutors] says I'm the greatest trouble he has in recitation, and has deducted for whispering frequently." On another occasion he reports: "Slept thro' sermon, hymn, prayer, read'g proclamation, and blessing. Pleasant! Fellows laughed at me a good deal." And later of a lecture: "Snoozed thro' it all comfortably."

Despite his troublesome conduct—and we must remember his extreme youth—Wentworth developed into a hardworking student whose performance improved markedly by his senior year. Extracts from his journals indicate the growing mastery of his studies: "President Quincy was present at our Livy recitation. Lucky. I never recited better."—"President Q. was present at our recitation in Herodotus. Got along decently."—"Went to President to get my marks. He wants me to behave well, so he says at least."[8] Higginson's hard work resulted in his election, as a junior, to Phi Beta Kappa, and he graduated second in his class. Still, undergraduate life at Harvard in the 1830s was not entirely a grind, as one of his notebook entries suggests: "Many of the class having become slightly boozy, made somewhat of a noise in prayers."[9]

III   *The Transcendental "Newness"*

During Higginson's undergraduate years, a new religious, philosophical, and literary movement swept through the college, and through America: the Transcendental "Newness." It was an indigenous form of American Romanticism. Theodore Parker and

Ralph Waldo Emerson were its principal New England spokesmen. The discovery of Emerson, Higginson later wrote, would be for any young man "a great event in life, but in the comparative conventionalism of the literature of that period it had the effect of a revelation."[10] Parker's sermons and Emerson's lectures and essays—*Nature* (1836), "The American Scholar" (1837), "The Divinity School Address" (1838), and "Self-Reliance" (1841)—expressed the basic faith of Transcendentalism, a faith in spiritual insight as the guide to truth, and in reliance on subjective feeling as the validation of reality. Transcendentalism subordinated history and tradition to the urgencies of the immediate present. It saw Nature as the symbol of the spiritual center of the universe and urged men to get in touch with that Divine Oversoul by listening to the inner voice.

The key to the period—as Emerson observed in "Historic Notes on Life and Letters in New England"—was that "mind had become aware of itself. Men grew reflective and intellectual. There was a new consciousness."[11] "The summer of 1839," as William Henry Channing remarked, "saw the full dawn of the Transcendental movement in New England." Channing defined it as "an assertion of the inalienable integrity of man, of the immanence of Divinity in instinct. In part, it was a reaction against Puritan Orthodoxy; in part, an effect of renewed study of the ancients, of Oriental Pantheists, of Plato and the Alexandrians, of Plutarch's *Morals*, Seneca and Epictetus; in part, the natural product of the culture of the place and time."[12]

The German Idealism of Kant, Jacobi, Fichte, and Novalis, reinforced by the teachings of Schelling, Hegel, Carlyle, and Schleiermacher, reinvigorated the "stunted stock of Unitarianism." And the result was "a vague yet exalting conception of the godlike nature of the human spirit." For these disciples of the "Newness"—Margaret Fuller, Channing, James Freeman Clarke, Orestes Brownson, the Ripleys, Emerson, Thoreau, and others—Transcendentalism was "a pilgrimage from the idolatrous world of creeds and rituals to the temple of the Living God in the soul. It was a putting to silence of tradition and formulas, that the Sacred Oracle might be heard through intuitions of the single-eyed and pure-hearted."[13]

Essentially a Romantic epistemology, Transcendentalism took as many forms as its individualistic adherents could devise, but they shared a common belief in "perpetual inspiration, the miraculous power of will, and a birthright to universal good." Each

Transcendentalist "sought to hold communion face to face with the unnameable Spirit of his spirit, and gave himself up to the embrace of nature's beautiful joy. . . ." The sense of sin and damnation, endemic in the vestigial Puritan culture of New England, was abandoned in favor of a belief in the essential goodness of humanity and in the possibility, by will and action, of fulfilling the imperatives of the self. Its maxims were "Trust, dare, and be; infinite good is ready for your asking; seek and find. All that your fellows can claim or need is that you should become, in fact, your highest self; fulfill, then, your ideal." Anti-institutionalists, they still banded together to effect social reforms and published their views in *The Dial, The Harbinger,* and *The Boston Quarterly Review.* A fellowship of the "like-minded," who disagreed more often than not, Transcendentalism was a brotherhood of free and independent thought and of a liberal and hopeful spirit.[14]

In its rejection of Christian doctrine, the "Newness" was, of course, heretical to orthodox belief, and Andrews Norton, Dexter Professor of Sacred Literature at the Divinity School, denounced it as "The Latest Form of Infidelity." But Higginson was strongly attracted to this current of religious radicalism. In one respect he was fortunate. Orthodox theology played little part in his religious education, which tended rather toward what Emerson called "the corpse-cold Unitarianism of Harvard College and Brattle Street."[15] Higginson was later to observe: "Greatly to my bliss, I escaped almost absolutely all those rigors of the old New England theology which have darkened the lives of so many. I never heard of the Five Points of Calvinism until maturity; never was converted, never experienced religion. We were expected to read the New Testament, but there was nothing enforced about the Old. . . . Even Sunday brought no actual terrors. . . . Compared with the fate of many contemporaries, what soothing and harmless chains were these!"[16]

As a consequence of his mother's religious liberalism, Wentworth Higginson found it easy to abandon the "pale negations" of conservative Unitarianism—with its orthodoxy of the historicity of miracles and reason—in favor of the emotional fervors of the Transcendental "Newness," which espoused the divinity of all men (not just of Jesus), the supernaturalism of all existence (not just that of biblical miracle), and the continuity of divine revelation (not merely that of the Scripture).

During his Harvard years, moreover, Higginson was very close to a gifted literary and social circle which included James Russell

Lowell and his fiancée, Maria White. Higginson was later to say that "if this circle of bright young people was not strictly a part of the Transcendental Movement, it was yet born of 'the Newness.' Lowell and Story, indeed, both wrote for 'The Dial,' and Maria White had belonged to Margaret Fuller's classes. There was, moreover, passing through the whole community a wave of that desire for a freer and more ideal life which made Story turn aside from his father's profession to sculpture, and made Lowell forsake law after his first client." The intellectual excitement of that era is suggested by Emerson's remark to Carlyle: "We are all a little wild here with numberless projects of social reform; not a reading man but has a draft of a new community in his waistcoat pocket." Higginson himself "longed at times to cut free from prescribed bondage" and to put himself "on more equal terms with that vast army of handworkers who were ignorant of much that I knew, yet could do so much that I could not."

Under the influence of the "Newness," Higginson developed "a project of going into the cultivation of peaches, an industry then prevalent in New England, but now practically abandoned,—thus securing freedom for study and thought by moderate labor of the hands." This project was contemplated in 1843, "two years before Thoreau tried a similar project with beans at Walden Pond; and also before the time when George and Burrill Curtis undertook to be farmers at Concord. . . . Such things were in the air, and even those who were not swerved by 'the Newness' from their intended pursuits were often greatly modified as to the way in which these were undertaken. . . ."[17]

IV *Poet or Pastor?*

After his graduation in 1841, Higginson's desire to cut himself free from his "prescribed bondage" was intensified by the Channing family, with whom he became intimate in Brookline, while he was tutoring the children of Stephen Higginson Perkins, his radical, freethinking cousin. Perkins and William Henry Channing, whom Emerson would call "the evil time's sole patriot" (for his opposition to the Mexican War), took Wentworth to the fiery abolition conventions in Boston, where he heard the "strange enthusiasm" of William Lloyd Garrison and Wendell Phillips put to the sublime service of defending human freedom and condemning slavery. Before long Higginson was devoted to abolitionism: "I had the ex-

citement of the great Abolition convention which I several times
attended. Got some settled views about abolition, and all but made
a speech." After a few more of these conventions, he recorded: "I
have got the run of slavery argumentation now and can talk
Abolitionism pretty well."[18]

Still hardly more than a boy, Wentworth was perplexed about his
vocation in life. One choice open to him was that of the poet. His
early poetical effusions—sonnets to Longfellow, Motherwell, Tennyson, and Sterling—reveal only a modest talent. But his poem on
the Sistine Madonna was the talk of Cambridge for a few weeks,
and, when Longfellow reprinted it in *The Estray*, Higginson was
aflame with the possibilities of a life devoted to poetry. Unfortunately, the ordinariness of New England life did not seem to
stimulate the creative impulse. Reading "Undine," he echoed the
plaint of young American Romantics at the poverty, for American
literature, of our lack of myth and legend: "Just now I heard a noise
outside the window and looked up in hopes it was Kühleborn—oh,
how dreadful it is to be in a land where there are no supernatural
beings visible—not even any traditions of them."[19] He imagined
himself to be the dreamy poet and sat up to all hours writing blank
verse. His diary records that when he read one poem to his family,
"they laughed at its sentimentality, which enraged me . . . went to
bed angry and feeling unappreciated. Resolved to show them no
more poetry."[20] His uncertainty about his poetic future appears in
his exclamation: "Oh, heavens, what I would not give to know
whether I really have that in me which will make a poet, or whether
I deceive myself and only possess a mediocre talent."[21]

After graduation, that summer in Brookline, he asked only for
"books and nature—and leisure and means to give myself up to
them and some one to share my ideas with, and I think I should be
perfectly happy." About this time he recorded himself as "overflow-
ing with mental energies—I will be Great if I can." He was still an
adolescent, however, as another nearby journal entry reveals: "I
made an Excursion (about ¼ 12) & attacked the 4 steel signs in the
neighborhood—no one suspecting but the girls. No danger—in
spite of the $50 reward."[22]

Wentworth's desire for "some one to share my ideas with" was a
problem from early adolescence onwards. As he noted in his diary:
"I don't believe there ever was a child in whom the sentimental was
earlier developed than in me." This "sentimentality" led him to
"rate" the young ladies of his acquaintance: "It is not exactly love I

feel towards M.C.D.—it is rather a *Platonic* affection, if there is any
such thing—or a *connubial* one." After escorting Papanti's "best
scholar and very agreeable girl" home from a dance, he entered in
his diary: "To bed at 11½. Smitten." Then later: "Felt sentimental and loafing. Oh, M.C.!" His mooning after the young ladies of
Cambridge came to be a problem for the dedicated student, for he
next records: "Dulcinea absent for which I am glad, for to have seen
her would have used me up for some days." And he lectures himself
in his diary about the unsettling effect on him of his susceptibility to
female charms. At the end of his sophomore year he records: "Look
out, Higginson, or your resolution . . . [to lead his class] will go to
grass!"[23]

His susceptibility to female charms made him extremely self-
conscious. Tall, skinny, and rather awkward, he compensated for his
personal "defects" by a studied dandyism. His diaries record his
satisfaction at appearing in public wearing a "black coat, new pants,
dark 'veskit,' blk stockings & pumps." Once he records "strutting"
after church to show off the "combination of gaiters and high
heels"; and he took satisfaction in the curling of his hair, which improved it. On another occasion he notes: "Promenaded the [Boston]
streets in my silk attire till 7." Then: "Took a walk after
church—my new pants perfect. . . . Walked out from Boston to
Cambridge. My new boots pinched my feet so I could hardly walk.
What did I do thereupon! Stopped at the Port, sat down, pulled
them off, and walked home barefoot. It was dark, remember."[24]

Thanks to his friendship with the Channings in Brookline, he met
Mary Channing, sister of William Ellery, the poet. She encouraged
his reading, and gradually Wentworth was led to explore the European literature on which the new American Romanticism was
based. He steeped himself in the writings of Madame de Staël, Victor Cousin, Benjamin Constant, Pierre Leroux, and Schubert. After
Emerson, he was most influenced by Jean Paul Richter, whose life
story made Higginson, at nineteen, a dreamer steeped in Nature,
committed on principle to poverty (he had no money, in any case),
and to a free life of independent studies.

One of his journal entries suggests the influence of Richter on his
conception of the future: "Spent the whole morning at
home—reading Richter's Life and meditating and made the day an
era in my life by fixing the resolution of not studying a
profession. . . . The resolve is perfectly settled and perfectly
tranquil with me, that I will come as near starving as Richter

did—that I will labor as intently and suffer as much—sooner than
violate my duty toward my Spiritual Life" and "to do my duty to
the world at large, in whatever manner I can best use my
talents. . . . For myself I believe and trust that I have got *above*
following Ambition as the leading motive. . . . For neither Wealth
nor Fame will, I trust, make me happy or satisfy me."[25]

V   Private Study in Cambridge

Higginson therefore returned to Cambridge, immersed himself in
nature and books—Newton, Ritter, Sismondi, Lamennais, Homer,
Hesiod, and "Emerson over and over."[26] His Cambridge period of
study in the early 1840s was "a nice oysterlike life with occasional
trips to Brookline and Boston."[27]

However, as his classmate O. B. Frothingham was later to
observe, "the Transcendentalist was by nature a reformer. He could
not be satisfied with men as they were. His doctrine of the
capacities of men, even in its most moderate statement, kindled to
enthusiasm his hope of change. However his disgust may have kept
him aloof for a time, his sympathy soon brought him back, and his
faith sent him to the front of the battle."[28] Higginson's private
study was too introverted, too unlikely to issue in the great work of
social reform. "I think on the whole that this life is not the right one
for me—I cannot live alone. Solitude may be good for study
sometimes, but not solitude in a crowd for a social-hearted person
like me. Here in my own pleasant room I seldom feel it, but when
outdoors I constantly feel the unpleasantness of having no common
interests in the life I lead and that of others."[29]

Communitarian cooperation offered one form of connection for
the social-hearted person. And Higginson frequently exchanged
views with members of the Brook Farm group of Utopian Socialists
who gathered at Elizabeth Peabody's foreign bookstore on West
Street. Higginson knew the Brook Farm founder, George Ripley,
and Charles Dana (later editor of the New York *Sun*). Nathaniel
Hawthorne was also then living in the community. Twice Higginson went out to Brook Farm. On his first visit, he thought it a
"pleasant looking place," where the combination of gentlemen and
laborers was "perfect." This impression did not last, however, for he
later records, "At the Community we saw a variety of dirty men,
boys and girls; and one or two clean ones."[30] In this complaint he
echoes Hawthorne, who felt that shoveling dung in the barnyard

seemed unlikely to elevate the soul. Still, Higginson was sympathetic to the theories on which the group was founded and retained a lifelong attraction to socialist thought.

More exciting than the Brook Farm doctrines were the radical sermons of Theodore Parker and James Freeman Clarke, who excoriated the materialism of the Boston merchants, condemned religious sectarianism, and denounced an economic and social order that tolerated slavery. Should Higginson attempt the ministry? The prospect was not encouraging, for he had no interest in Christian doctrine and felt the liturgical forms of church life to be strangling to the free life of the Spirit. But his vocation as a poet was deserting him. "The idea of poetic genius is now utterly foreign to me and I cannot conceive at all now the feeling that underlay my whole life two years ago. I must be content to enjoy instead of creating poetry."[31]

As he struggled to find his vocation, his journals record his uncertainty: "What destiny is intended for me I cannot tell—not to go in the beaten track I am sure. I cannot express how strongly I long to come out and obtain a working place among men. How my ability will second my wishes I know not, but some things are in every one's power—to live a true, sincere, earnest, independent life. Of this I think daily and hourly. . . ." "I feel there is no man too small to be useful so he be true and bold. . . . I am an enthusiast now, I know. So much the better. Whoever was in the highest degree useful without being such?"[32] Still he wavered between the ministry and the literary life and private studies. Periodically he was overcome with fits of deep depression, which alternated with his basically optimistic spirit. By an act of will he triumphed over his depression: "Assumed my Cambridge state of mind. . . . I certainly intend to try—and not give way to the causeless melancholy I have occasionally fallen into heretofore. . . ." And he "resolved to wake up from my dreams and work."[33]

Under the influence of Parker and Clarke, Higginson eventually found himself "gravitating toward what was then called the 'liberal' ministry."[34] Some of Higginson's Transcendental friends thought that divinity study was a defection from the free life of the self. Had not Emerson himself resigned from his pulpit in 1832? Higginson knew that if his ministry could be sufficiently secular, if his preaching could be devoted to Christian ethics and to social reform, a pastorate could be an avenue of useful service to humanity. He therefore returned to Harvard.

VI *At the Divinity School*

J. G. Palfrey, then dean, described the Harvard Divinity School as composed of "mystics, skeptics, and dyspeptics."[35] Professors Ezra Styles Gannett, Andrews Norton, and Andrew Peabody were the principal dyspeptics, largely because of the heretical strains of Transcendentalism infusing the student body in the 1840s. Norton told his classes that "the human mind has no inherent faculty of perception in the sphere of facts which transcends the cognizance of the senses," and he argued that "intuition can inform us of nothing but what exists in our own minds; it is therfore a mere absurdity to maintain that we have an intuitive knowledge of the truths of religion." Norton's Lockean rationalism ran counter to that "strong mystical tendency" Higginson recognized in himself. It led him, like Schleiermacher, to think that "Religion . . . is a feeling obviously—exists as a feeling in our mind. Reason can do nothing itself but . . . accept revelation."[36]

Although formal theology had little interest for Higginson, he exercised himself in defending intuition as the avenue to truth. Insight without action, however, was useless. And he was critical of even the liberal professors, like Convers Francis, who theorized endlessly and amalgamated "the most opposite views into a tasteless transcendental mush." Transcendentalism, Higginson felt, lacked an adequate sense of the reality of evil (Emerson had called it the mere privation of good) and of the necessity of acting in the world so as to effect social amelioration. Everywhere in history, he wrote, he saw "the same story of the power of the individual soul, and the one great man—& when I look to the present & see how never was this man more needed, never was there a time a leader of men more wanted—& know from the past how glorious the power of such a leader: then I feel called to the work [by] the energetic & earnest powers within me." His ambition was to be "guiding, governing, pointing out the true course to those who cannot find it unaided—& adding to this the moral force of a disinterested philanthropy."[37]

Meanwhile, he steeped himself in the political argument, then raging, over the Mexican War and the admission to the Union of Texas, a slave state. What should be his role? How could he become a leader? "A pure earnest aim is not enough," he wrote. "Intellectual as well as moral armor must be bright for I know I shall have to sustain a warfare. I feel that if I do justice to my own powers (i.e., if

I do my duty) I cannot remain in the background. . . . Preaching alone I should love, but I feel inwardly that something more will be sought of me—An aesthetic life—how beautiful—but the life of a Reformer, a People's Guide 'battling for the right'—glorious, but, oh how hard!"[38] He therefore attended meetings in Faneuil Hall and composed verses about the Texas question for the *Liberty News*, the *Free State Rally*, and the *Liberator*. To his mother he wrote: "I have pretty much concluded that a consistent Abolitionist (which last every person who thinks and feels must be whether nominally or not) must choose between the Liberty Party and the Disunion Party. I don't like the dilemma at all, but fear I must come to it. . . . In the Liberty Bell which appears in a week at the Faneuil Hall Anti-Slavery Fair will be a sonnet of mine which may rather astonish some of my friends. Do not be afraid of seeing my name [signed] to pieces in papers."[39]

Meanwhile the "everlasting dogma, talk, talk talk, but no cooperation in good works"—which he thought characteristic of the Divinity School—led him to drop out of school. "Oh, I keep asking who is there to go on with me to the aid of liberal Christianity?" He was moved by the public witness of escaped slaves and the logic of the abolitionists' position. He thought he might become the poet of social reform, if not a practical politician. In January 1846, he recorded his "final self-enrollment in the ranks of the American Non-Jurors or Disunion Abolitionists" and his determination not only not to vote for any officer who must take oath to support the U.S. Constitution, but also to use whatever means may lie in my power to promote the Dissolution of the Union. . . . To Disunion I now subscribe in the full expectation that a time is coming which may expose to obloquy and danger even the most insignificant of the adherents to such a cause."[40]

In 1845 he reconsidered the value of "being regularly authorized to preach and the desirableness of being associated with a special set of young men." In his reapplication for admission to the Divinity School, he told the faculty that he had "abandoned much that men call belief," but was "disposed to see in Love and Spiritual Trust the only basis of Christian Life within or Christian Union without. . . ." He felt that he had "a gospel to preach" and was "ready to preach it."[41]

The faculty was persuaded by the earnestness of his appeal, Higginson was readmitted, and he threw himself once more into divinity studies, finding excitement in reading German biblical scholarship, exploring the early history of the Trinity, debating the true use of the Scriptures, and testing every dogma in terms of his radical, nondoctrinaire point of view. "Nothing keeps a man so fresh," he told his mother, "as abolitionism and kindred propensities, I observe."[42]

He had no doubts about his schoolwork, but he was in a quandary over whether his radical ideas would be tolerated by a conventional congregation of Christians. Especially he wondered whether his view of Christ—"as in the highest sense a *natural* character, divine as being in the highest sense human," would be "acceptable to people." He could not make up his mind "whether my radicalism will be the ruin of me or not."[43] Meanwhile, he preached in West Cambridge, Walpole, and Newburyport, in order to judge his chance of "obtaining a position & influence as a a preacher which may make it worthwhile for me to devote my life to it."[44]

On Visitation Day, July 16, 1847, Higginson preached a public sermon on "The Clergy and Reform." In the presence of the reverend clergy and laity of Boston, Cambridge, and Harvard—Parker, W. H. Channing, Samuel May, John Weiss, and Edward Everett Hale, among others—Higginson deplored the division between the clergy and the secular reformers (like Garrison and Phillips), and condemned the ministers for upholding the status quo and for failing to guide the social and moral regeneration of the world. The true reformers, he announced, would disregard the status quo, abhor moral relativism, "refer . . . to an *absolute* standard, point to a possible future and condemn the present. . . ." For Higginson the orthodox clergy had failed, for their priesthood was "built on Form & Doctrine, not on practical life!" Though the sermon was "a rock of offence" to many of his listeners, Higginson was widely praised and he became a household name overnight. Still, the real issue remained—whether the clergy and the secular reformers could unite in "the Christlike spirit of love & moral indignation,"[45] in order to rectify social evils of slavery. The First Religious Society of Newburyport apparently saw in Higginson a promising clergyman, for he was called to the ministry there. Ostensibly a Unitarian church, the congregation in fact bore no denominational name, and since it appeared disposed to tolerate Higginson's liberalism, he accepted the call. Then he married Mary Channing. His education was complete. He was twenty-four.

VII *The Ministry of Christian Radicalism*

Though the First Religious Society of Newburyport was un-prepared for the radicalism of its new young pastor, the pulpit had been vacant for a year and the church leaders could not guess how far Higginson could go in preaching "real Parker Sermons." New-buryport in the 1840s was a conservative village dominated by wealthy businessmen and sea captains, some of whom had earlier engaged in the African slave trade.

At the beginning of his pastorate, Higginson was direct but not inflammatory in his remarks to the conservative congregation of five hundred members. Yet his views on the Mexican War, the Polk ad-ministration, temperance, antislavery, and the materialism of businessmen satisfied James Freeman Clarke's charge at Higgin-son's ordination on September 15, 1847: "You cannot please everybody,—perhaps not anybody; still you may please your own conscience and God."[46]

Higginson pleased his own conscience. To one of his cor-respondents he wrote: "They [the parishioners] manifest regard for us only by full and attentive presence at church—certainly the most agreeable way, but queer. Not a particle of *petting*. Rather afraid of us, in fact, Mary thinks—as if we were handsome spotted panthers, good to look at and roaring finely—something to be proud of, perhaps—but not to be approached incautiously, or too near; except by a few familiar ones. . . . I have not yet found one who approves the war or disapproves free speech on the minister's part and I begin to feel somewhat confident that they will stand the trials I have ready for them. . . . I have talked very plainly in private."[47]

As his public talk became plainer, the Newburyport *Herald* began to attack him as "a young man of much intellectual and moral power," who seemed to be "tinctured with those radical and imaginative notions . . . which would fain seek to govern society at large more wisely than God has seen fit to guide it ever since the dawn of creation."[48]

Though antislavery was Higginson's chief cause, he was active in other issues then enrolled under the banner of the "Sisterhood of Reforms"—some of them, like his opposition to capital punishment, less objectionable to the Whigs of Newburyport than abolition. Among these practical causes was the temperance crusade. The effect of his sermons on the degradation of drink is evident in Mary's remark to a correspondent: "W.'s Temperance Sermon which he repeated last Sunday eve—has already done good—*three* establishments are to be closed in consequence."[49] Here was morality translated into action, and action was what Higginson above all craved. Action meant politics, and Higginson's pleasure in the politics of reform was intense. As he told his mother: "Last Tuesday and Wednesday I went to the State Temperance Convention; the best part of a Convention is the preliminary meeting when the wires are pulled and all the real fighting done. I was in the thick of it."[50]

Another cause enlisting his energies was organized labor, then agitating in behalf of a state bill for a ten-hour day. He also established "an evening school for the adult education of the working people, many of whom had little or no schooling, even the native born. It was Higginson's belief," as Howard N. Meyer has suggested, that "with education and a better understanding of the nature of the world in which they lived these people would find ways to help themselves."[51]

But, next to abolition, Higginson's chief cause was the rights of women, especially equal educational opportunity and the right to vote. As he told Mary, he thought it "a monstrous absurdity to talk of a democratic government and universal suffrage and yet exclude one-half the inhabitants without any ground of incapacity to plead." And, he added, "I think there is no possible argument on the other side excepting prejudice."[52]

After the turn of the century, looking back at all of his labors in behalf of the Sisterhood of Reforms, and noting that he had signed the call in 1850 for the first national convention for women's rights, he observed: "Of all the movements in which I ever took part, except the antislavery agitation, this last-named seems to me the most important; nor have I ever wavered in the opinion announced by Wendell Phillips, that it is 'the grandest reform yet launched upon the century, as involving the freedom of one half the human race.' "[53] No wonder then that Higginson was popular with the blacks, the immigrants, the laboring men, the working women, and the devout abolitionists of Newburyport. Harriet Prescott Spofford, one of the girls who taught in Higginson's evening school for workers, later recalled: " 'Mr. Higginson was like a great archangel to us all then, and there were so many of us! Coming into the humdrum life of the town, he was like someone from another star.' "[54]

But Higginson was not popular with conservatives in his congregation. Temperance was one thing, but abolition was another, and increasingly his antislavery sermons estranged the leaders of the church. In Newburyport he had found himself, he later observed, "at once the associate of all that was most reputable in the town, in virtue of my functions; and also, by the fatality of temperament, of all that was most radical."[55] In October 1847, for example, the Essex County Anti-Slavery Society held its meeting in Newburyport. Higginson called this meeting to the attention of the congregation in a sermon based on the text "Behold the men who have turned the world upside down are come hither also." The sermon urged his parishioners to attend this antislavery meeting. Many evidently did, for he reported that there had been "much discussion on the subject this week and I feel entirely satisfied with the success of my effort—which has not, so far as I know, excited any opposition. At all events I have defined my position."[56] His position became even clearer in the autumn of 1848, when he accepted the nomination of the Free Soil party for Congress. The wealthy Whigs in his congregation were dismayed at Higginson's politicization, which took the partisan form of denouncing the Whig nominee, General Zachary Taylor, as a slaveholder. Higginson supported Garrisonian abolitionism. To his brother, Higginson wrote: "You have probably seen my nomination for Congress. I did all I could to get [John Greenleaf] Whittier nominated, but he obstinately declined, and it was he who proposed my name. . . . It will hurt my popularity in Newburyport for they call it ambition &c.—but I trust that time will do me justice."[57]

Taylor swept the election, however, and Higginson went down to defeat. Higginson afterward reproached his congregation for having elected a slaveholding president, and after hearing Frederick Douglass describe the evil of slavery, he said that he felt "as if I were a recreant to humanity, to let one Sunday pass in the professed preaching of Christianity, and leave the name of SLAVERY unmentioned. . . . And so help me God I never will again."[58]

He never did. The consequence of his devotion to abolition soon made itself felt: church attendance dwindled. "Several of the leading and *richest* men, who talked of leaving last winter, are resolved upon it now; minor ones propose to follow; and even my friends feel grave when they look forward and fancy a gradual procession of staunch members retiring one by one, leaving at least a dozen come-outers in the gallery and one more in the pulpit." Some of his women parishioners continued to support him; but, as he told his mother, "My (Masculine) supporters are in a numerical minority and a woeful pecuniary minority."[59] And to Samuel Johnson he wrote, "Not a dozen are really opposed to me, but they have all the *wealth*. Oh Christian Church!"[60]

In September 1848, the ax fell. "The case was perfectly simple," he told his mother. "Mr. W. distinctly stated that they had no fault to find with me personally, they liked and respected me; they were always interested in my preaching; they had no complaint as to pastoral matters; the only thing he had ever heard mentioned was Slavery and Politics; my position as an Abolitionist they could not bear. This, he admitted, could not be altered; and he tacitly recognized that I had but one course to pursue."[61]

Unacceptable to his influential congregants, Higginson submitted his resignation, acknowledging the failure of the pastoral "experiment," but observing to his congregation that "an empty pulpit has often preached louder than a living minister."[62]

For the next two years, Higginson remained nearby, living in Artichoke Mills, supporting himself and Mary through a bequest from his grandfather and by lecturing. He consoled his mother with the example of his clerical Puritan forefathers, noting a remark in "Dr. Young's Chronicles that when Francis Higginson, the ancient, became a non-conformist 'he was accordingly excluded from his pulpit; but a lectureship was established for him, in which he was maintained by the voluntary contributions of the inhabitants'; so I have good precedents."[63] He later felt that his struggle on behalf of slaves was part of the constitutional character of the family: "There was, perhaps, some tendency that way in the blood, for I rejoice to recall the fact that after Judge Sewall, in 1700, had published his noted tract against slavery, called 'The Selling of Joseph,' the first protest against slavery in Massachusetts, he himself testified six years later, 'Amidst the frowns and hard words I have met with for this Undertaking, it is no small refreshment to me that I can have the Learned Reverend and Aged Mr. Higginson for Abetter.' "[64]

Meanwhile, he was active in the Newburyport Lyceum, arranging and publicizing lectures and entertaining speakers in his home. The naturalist Louis Agassiz, the great preacher Henry Ward Beecher, Senator Charles Sumner, and the abolitionist Lucy Stone—"as unshrinking and self-possessed as a loaded cannon,"[65]—were some of his houseguests. On another occasion he noted: "Mr. Emerson comes on Friday and will stop here—as will also probably the minor star, Dr. Holmes, the week after. 'T is a nice way of seeing great people, for they can't well be otherwise than complaisant when you rescue them from a dirty tavern and give them hominy for breakfast."[66]

During this period he was unable to reconcile himself to "the recurring *forms* even of worship, still less those connected with church organization."[67] He told his friend Sam Longfellow that he found "everywhere ground of discontent in all our existing religious and ecclesiastical forms." Doctrine and liturgy, he felt, belonged to the past; and however "plastic to new Life" they might be, the "dawning Age of Faith" demanded "a fresh organization to vivify."[68] But what kind of organization? Even the non-denominational churches like that in Newburyport were too rigid for his purposes. And he observed to his Aunt Nancy, "as regards *preaching* proper, I have no sort of doubt of its being my mission—in some form or other—that is *speaking* to men, in the pulpit or elsewhere. . . . But enough of churches and preachers and future botherations; what trifles they all seem when Spring is opening and the tardy blue anemones are almost ready to open their blue eyes."[69]

During this period at Artichoke Mills, Higginson immersed himself once more in nature. He was one of the first to recognize Thoreau's *A Week on the Concord and Merrimack Rivers* as a great work of Transcendental naturalism. He even went out to Concord expressly to meet its author. Thoreau, he noted, "is more human and polite than I supposed, and said he had heard Mr. Emerson speak of me; he is a little bronzed spare man; he makes lead pencils with his father on Monday and Tuesday and was in the midst of work. On other days he surveys land, both mathematically and meditatively; lays out houselots in Haverhill and in the moon." He remarked that Thoreau talked "sententiously and originally; his manner is the most unvarying facsimile of Mr. Emerson's, but his thoughts are quite his own. . . . He does not seem particularly affected by applause, but rather by his own natural egotism. I find nobody who enjoys his book as I do (this I did not tell him)." And he concluded, "I saw his mother, a gaunt and elderly Abolitionist who had read my Thanksgiving sermon with comfort, and told me anecdotes of 'Henry's' ways which are more domestic and filial than one would suppose."[70]

In the spring of 1849, life at the Mills seemed idyllic, and Higginson indulged himself in prose poems to nature's beauty: "That subterranean fire of which Thoreau speaks seems very near the surface;

the buds and Catkins are unusually large; we bring in older blooms, in their winter dress, stiff and black, nearly an inch long, and the water soon brings them out, till they droop to long yellow tresses and then let fall their powdery seeds. We have tried the birch catkins also, but their time is later and they have not yet come out. Meanwhile even outdoors the little muddy lichen-cups rise under the snow, and overhead the oaks and beeches have still a perpetual summer in their withered leaves. There are no pines very near us, but the groves on the point across the river show now in their native greenness, now white with snow, now green with mist."[71]

But however rich Nature might be as a source of sensual and contemplative satisfaction, Higginson craved action in the human arena. When the Fugitive Slave Law was passed in 1850, he stood for Congress as a Free Soil party candidate. Thoreau's "Civil Disobedience" (1848) counseled that "Those who call themselves abolitionists should at once effectually withdraw their support, both in person and property, from the government of Massachusetts,"[72] and Thoreau had gone to jail to dramatize that withdrawal. Higginson admired the nonviolent resistance of Thoreau and the pacificism of Whittier and of the Garrisonian abolitionists. But he went further, telling his neighbors that since the Fugitive Slave Law "must . . . yield to a higher law,"[73] right-thinking Massachusetts men would refuse to catch or return escaped slaves. The Newburyport *Union* accused him of openly advocating "the nullification of the laws of the land, when they do not correspond with his individual opinions."[74] But in his "address to the Voters," referring to the fugitive-slave provision of the Compromise Act of 1850, he said "DISOBEY IT . . . and show our good citizenship by taking the legal consequences!"[75] He abhorred bloodshed, he told his would-be constituents. But in "terrible times" it became "necessary to speak of bloodshed." When push came to shove, he warned, "it is hard to say where a man must stop in defending his inalienable rights."[76]

Several test cases of the Fugitive Slave Law inflamed Higginson's antagonism to this "immoral legislation" in the 1850s, and shoved him in the direction of that violence he so abhorred. One case involved an escaped slave named Sims, who was arrested in Boston and returned to Georgia, to be publicly whipped. Higginson was dismayed with the "great want of preparation on our part for this revolutionary work,"[77] and he tried to persuade Marshal Tukey of Newburyport of the immorality of pursuing escaped slaves. And to his classmate Charles Devons, then a United States marshal, he wrote:

For myself there is something in the thought of assisting to return to slavery a man guilty of no crime but a colored skin [at which] every thought of my nature rebels in . . . horror. I think not now of the escaped slave, though he has all my sympathies, but of the free men and women who are destined to suffer for this act. And I almost feel as if the nation of which we have boasted were sunk in the dust forever, now that justice and humanity are gone; and as if the 19th century were the darkest of all the ages.[78]

In the meantime his powerful oratory and his moral energy became known to the leaders of the Free Church at Worcester. He had supposed himself "to have given up preaching forever," but the Worcester congregation—"with no church membership or communion service, not calling themselves Christian, but resembling . . . [modern] ethical societies"—offered Higginson "a new sphere of reformatory action."[79]

During his Worcester pastorate (1852 - 1858), Higginson resumed the ministry of nondenominational ethical Christianity based on man's "intuition" of "the great Law of Nature," God's love, manifest in the humanity of Jesus. In practical affairs, he supported the ten-hour bill, land reform, penal legislation, temperance, antislavery, and women's rights—all much more popular causes in Worcester, a workingman's town.

In 1853, he helped to organize the World Temperance Convention in New York City. Since he loved to be in the thick of convention politics, where the wires are pulled, he moved the appointment of Susan B. Anthony to the Committee on Arrangements. Thereupon, the convention disintegrated into an uproar of hissing and catcalls, for Miss Anthony was widely despised as a feminist radical. During the uproar Higginson resigned from the committee, warning that no World Temperance Convention could possibly be effective which excluded representatives of half the human race. He led the walkout which resulted in the eventual formation of a "*Whole* World's Temperance Convention," featuring the support of some of the great radicals of his day—Elizabeth Cady Stanton, Susan B. Anthony, Lucy Stone, Lucretia Mott, Abby Foster, Phillips, Garrison, Parker, and Horace Greeley, among others. Higginson was the unanimous choice as its chairman.[80] But the

Sims case and others like it rankled deep in his heart. All he asked of
fate, he recorded in his diary, was "one occasion worth bursting the
door for—an opportunity to get beyond this boy's play."[81]

VIII   Resistance to the Fugitive Slave Law

That opportunity came to Higginson, then thirty, on Wednesday,
May 24, 1854, when he received word from Samuel May that
Anthony Burns, an escaped slave, had been seized in Boston and
that a public protest was scheduled at Faneuil Hall on Friday night.
Higginson immediately went to Boston and closeted himself with
the Vigilance Committee. Composed of Higginson, Parker, Phillips,
Samuel Gridley Howe, Austin Bearse, Martin Stowell, and William
Kemp, the committee debated a forcible rescue of the slave Burns.
Most opposed any violence, but they agreed to formulate a plan on
Friday at the Faneuil Hall demonstration.

Meanwhile, Stowell privately urged Higginson to action, citing
their ineffectuality in the Sims affair. On Friday night, while the
crowds were filling up the hall, Higginson, agreeing that they must
take *some* action, purchased a dozen handaxes from a nearby
hardware store, hid them in the office of Henry Bowditch, across
from the Court House, and went over to Faneuil Hall. Higginson
and Stowell then presented to the committee their plan for an
assault on the Court House, while the meeting was in session, on
the ground that the police and deputies would be expecting trouble
after the demonstration broke up. Howe and Kemp agreed to the
plan. Parker also consented, although in the noise and confusion he
misunderstood the plans. Phillips's consent could not be secured, as
he was lost somewhere in the crowd. Austin Bearse opposed the
idea. While Parker harangued the Boston crowd ("Fellow citizens of
Virginia"—"No, no!"), Higginson and Stowell slipped out of the
hall, returned to the office of Henry Bowditch, and Higginson dis-
tributed the handaxes. Stowell and a few others were armed with
pistols as well. Meanwhile Phillips had begun to speak at the hall.
At a prearranged time, Higginson's "plant" interrupted the
meeting to announce that Negroes were already storming the Court
House and attempting a rescue. At this, Faneuil Hall dissolved into
an uproar and the sympathetic crowd surged for the exits and headed for the Court House.

Higginson's men, hearing the tumult of the approaching crowd,
led the assault on the Court House with stones, axes, and a

fourteen-foot battering ram. Higginson had been a detached planner and director of these events. But in the excitement of the moment, he threw down his umbrella, seized hold of the battering ram himself, and helped to smash in the door. Almost immediately he found himself pushed inside the darkened Court House, where the guards were laying about with clubs and cutlasses. He and a black collaborator were momentarily trapped inside, and in the melee Higginson was gashed in the face by a cutlass. When the mob fell back, Higginson roared out to those behind him, "You cowards, will you desert us now?" In the darkness and confusion, someone answered with a pistol shot, killing a Court House guard. The mob was paralyzed by the gunfire. A number of those outside, including Stowell, were arrested by a swarm of police, and in the confusion Higginson somehow contrived to recover his umbrella and escape into the crowd.

Taking refuge in W. F. Channing's house, Higginson wrote Mary that "there has been an attempt at rescue and failed. I am not hurt except a scratch on the face which will prevent me from doing anything more about it, lest I be recognized."[82]

Little more could be done in any event, since the U.S. marshal brought in federal troops to guard Anthony Burns. Back in Worcester the next day, Higginson—his wound bandaged—was greeted as a hero by a throng of cheering supporters. He told Mary that he had heard "rumors of my arrest, but hardly expect it. If true, I hope no U.S. Officer will be sent up, for I cannot answer for his life in the streets of Worcester."[83] Meanwhile—though he felt this to be "the greatest step in Anti-Slavery which Massachusetts has ever taken"—he urged the Vigilance Committee to provide "assistance to the family of the man shot, supposing it to be so arranged as to show no contrition on our part, for a thing in which we had no responsibility, but simply to show that we have no war with women and children."[84]

Burns, however, was lost to the Slave Power. Not even the fifty thousand people who lined the Boston streets, booing and hissing, could obstruct the two thousand armed guards who conducted the prisoner to the boat which returned him to the South.

Richard Henry Dana confided his surprise at Higginson's conduct to his journal: "I knew his ardor and courage," he wrote, "but I hardly expected a married man, a clergyman, and a man of education to lead the mob."[85] Few could have been more surprised than Higginson himself. He was living in a dream state, like that during the Sims affair, when he had confessed: "It is strange to find one's self outside of established institutions; to be obliged to lower one's voice and conceal one's purposes," and "to see law and order, police and military, on the wrong side, and find good citizenship a duty."[86]

In the pulpit on Sunday after the Court House attack, Higginson defined the duty of good citizenship in "Massachusetts in Mourning." Preaching on the text of Jeremiah 15:12—"Shall iron break the northern iron and steel?"—he declared that the time for words was past, that resistance to tyranny was obedience to God, and that, for himself, "I can only make life worth living for, by becoming a revolutionist."[87]

Though Higginson warmed to the prospect of his trial on the charge of riot, and prepared a defense based on the immorality of the Fugitive Slave Law, he was never tried. The first grand jury in Boston found no cause to indict, and, though the second brought charges, the indictment was quashed on a technicality. Many years later, he observed that it seemed "almost incredible that any condition of things should have turned honest American men into conscientious law-breakers."[88] But the shameful compromise of 1850, with its Fugitive Slave Law, created the conditions for a guerrilla warfare, fought by men of democratic principle, of Christian conscience, based on faith in a law they held higher than that of the United States in 1854.

IX   Border Warfare in Kansas

A further field for underground warfare against the evils of slavery opened up in Kansas during the 1850s. In the contest over whether that territory would be slave or free, many of the Free Soil settlers in Kansas were being victimized by the advocates of slavery from Missouri, the "border ruffians." Higginson supported the recruitment of men, arms, and ammunition for Free Soil Northerners wishing to emigrate to Kansas, and even went west to report on the welfare of the New England men who had settled there. His "Letters from Kansas" depict the open insurrection constantly threatening, as marauding bands of Southerners plundered the wagon trains and settlements of the Northerners. He rode shotgun with a wagon train bound across the prairie for Topeka, telling his mother: "Imagine me also patrolling as one of the guards for an hour every night, in high boots amid the dewy grass, rifle in

hand and revolver in belt." Here was manly action aplenty. But fortunately no marauders laid siege to the wagon train, although
"once, in the day time, the whole company charged upon a band of
extremely nude Indians, taking them for Missourians."[89]
While in Lawrence, Higginson preached on the text of Nehemiah
4:14: "Be not ye afraid of them: remember the Lord, which is great
and terrible, and fight for your brethren, your sons and daughters,
your wives and your houses." The power of his sermons spread his
reputation through the settlements, and his life was continually
threatened.[90] In Kansas, Higginson found the living revolution in
behalf of the freedom he so earnestly desired.
John Brown, the instrument of that revolution, approached
Higginson in the winter of 1858, and requested money for his
"secret service." Brown was about to realize what he called "the
perfecting of BY FAR the most *important* undertaking of my whole
life."[91] He was necessarily secretive about his "undertaking," but
Higginson understood him to intend the rescue of fugitive slaves in
Virginia and the transport of them to safety in Canada.

X *Harper's Ferry*

The plan seemed unobjectionable, and between early 1858 and
October 1859, the "Secret Six"—Higginson, Parker, Howe, G. L.
Stearns, Frank Sanborn, and Gerrit Smith—conspired to raise
money for old Osawatomie to effect this plan. Their dream explod-
ed in gunfire and smoke on October 18, 1859, when Brown led a
small band of followers in a futile assault on the federal arsenal at
Harper's Ferry, Virginia. Frank Sanborn headed immediately for
Canada, and was soon followed by Stearns and Howe. Smith
entered an insane asylum. Parker was then dying of a terminal
illness in Italy. Only Higginson remained in the country, in the expectation of arrest for his part in supporting what had turned out to
be an insane scheme. Higginson expressed sorrow that Brown's
Northern supporters had not been at Harper's Ferry. During the
trial he rode down to North Elba, New York, to persuade Brown's
wife of the desirability of an armed attempt to rescue her husband.
But Brown would not hear of an escape attempt and so, after his
trial, was executed on December 2. Nor were Higginson's efforts to
rescue Brown's confederates any more successful. Higginson was
never arrested for supporting Brown's "undertaking"; nor, strange-
ly, was he ever called to Washington to testify before the Mason

Committee, even though his complicity was known to the United States government. The Congress, he concluded, where "white men are concerned," would "yield before the slightest resistance," and dared not try to arrest him in Worcester.[92]

XI   Commanding a Black Regiment

Well before 1857, Higginson had insisted that the irreconcilable differences between the North and the South required "the expulsion of the Slave States from the confederation in which they have been an element of discord, danger, and disgrace."[93] Consequently, in January of that year, he called to order the Massachusetts Disunion Convention to lay the groundwork, whether by peaceful or violent means, for that expulsion. At the time, Higginson, Phillips, Garrison, and their allies were denounced by conservatives as wild-eyed fanatics and lunatic demagogues. Even as late as the spring of 1861, these abolitionists were often the target of violent crowds, and Higginson and his friends were often forced to serve as armed bodyguards for Phillips, Emerson, and Parker at public meetings in Boston. But the firing on Fort Sumter in April changed all that, resolving the North into a troubled unanimity and vindicating, finally, the political foresight of the antislavery reformers.

In a series of articles in the *Atlantic* on "Nat Turner's Insurrection," "Denmark Vesey," "Haitian Emigration," and "Ordeal by Battle," Higginson prophesied the eventual emancipation of the slaves, whatever the outcome of the war. But he remained indecisive about his own role in the conflict, contenting himself with "a quiet life with literature and nature,"[94] for when the war broke out—after a decade of abolitionist exhortation, riot, and gun-running—he was drained of physical and spiritual energy. Nor was he any longer the *young* firebrand, being thirty-seven at the commencement of hostilities.

Nevertheless, the reasons for this hesitation at enlisting were complex and constitute no discredit to his character. First, he was, after all, a Christian minister who felt unequipped for military service. Second, his wife Mary was a total invalid, and he felt responsible for her welfare. But, more important, Higginson was deeply suspicious of the aims of the federal government in prosecuting the war. He had no wish to put down the Southern secession if Washington were not committed to the abolition of slavery. (In fact, the Emancipation Proclamation was not issued until 1863.) Disunion, he had always felt, might be the best course for the North, and the prospect of a return to the *status quo ante* was intolerable.

As the weeks passed into months, however, Higginson became more and more restive. Consequently, in August 1862, he raised a group of Worcester volunteers and was appointed captain of a company of the 51st Massachusetts Regiment. During that fall Higginson mastered the manuals and drilled his men. But shortly after he began to prepare his company, Higginson received an offer from General Rufus Saxton, Military Governor of the Southern Department, which changed the course of his military career.

In November, Higginson learned that the U.S. Army was considering the creation of a regiment of freed South Carolina slaves. There was considerable doubt among military strategists that these ex-slaves could be trained properly or that they could be counted on under fire. Higginson had few reservations, believing that the liberated blacks would fight for their freedom even more resolutely than their white Northern liberators. Who was more appropriate to lead them? In mid-November, he went to South Carolina and, under General Saxton, Colonel Higginson took command of the First South Carolina Volunteers, the first regiment of ex-slaves in the Union army.

A full discussion of Higginson's military career must be deferred until the analysis of *Army Life in a Black Regiment*. Nevertheless, it is worth noting here that Higginson had the distinction of organizing, administering, and leading into battle a regiment that conquered Jacksonville, Florida, in March 1863, and liberated hundreds of slaves from the plantations along the Edisto River in the interior of South Carolina. On one of his upriver patrols, in July 1863, Higginson was wounded by a concussion of shellfire which shattered the pilothouse of the boat. Though the injury was outwardly slight, his constitution, enfeebled perhaps by the fevers of malaria, did not respond to treatment satisfactorily. The army discharged him in April 1864 with a medical disability. He returned home to Massachusetts and a hero's welcome. He and his men, he later wrote in *Army Life in a Black Regiment*, "had touched the pivot of the war. . . . Till the blacks were armed, there was no guarantee of their freedom. It was their demeanor under arms that shamed the nation into recognizing them as men."[95]

XII   *The Radical in Peacetime*

On his discharge, Higginson and his wife Mary returned to Newport, Rhode Island, then becoming a watering place for the
wealthy. They did not move in the social circles of the summer
parvenus,[96] but were intimate with "the whole 'Atlantic' force" of
writers who had settled there: Mrs. Julia Ward Howe, author of
"The Battle Hymn of the Republic"; Helen Hunt Jackson, later the
author of *Mercy Philbrick's Choice* (1876) and *Ramona* (1884); John
La Farge, artist and future author of *Considerations on Painting*
(1895) and *An Artist's Letters from Japan* (1897); and other
members of the Town and Country Club.

In Newport, Higginson chaired the school committee, which
abolished "separate but equal" Negro schools in the town; he
organized the town library corporation and became one of its direc-
tors; he founded a local gymnasium and taught a large class in
calisthenics and physical culture; he fostered the work of the Sons of
Temperance; and several times he attended and spoke at woman's
suffrage conventions in Washington and Cleveland.

During the Reconstruction era, Higginson labored in behalf of
Negro enfranchisement, opposed the conciliation of the treasonous
political and military leaders of the South, and attacked the softness
of President Andrew Johnson and others who wished to bind up the
nation's wounds by restoring power "to the former lords of
Southern soil" who wished only to reestablish "slavery under the
name of 'Apprenticeship.'" Still, he doubted that reconstruction
politics would change men's hearts. He noted sadly that "We can
make no sudden changes in the constitution of men either at the
North or South. I do not look to see in this generation, a race of
Southern white men who shall do justice to the Negro."[97]

In addition, he had become deeply fatigued by the whole
antislavery-abolitionist-reconstruction movement. In 1865 he was
offered a job as agent for the Freedman's Aid Society in New
England, but declined, observing: "I do not want to give any more
years of my life exclusively to those people now, as much as I am attached to them." The work of liberating blacks, he concluded,
could not be accomplished in his lifetime; and, though he continued to support it, he felt that he could not lead the freedman's
cause any longer. He eventually urged on blacks that patience
which had sustained them through slavery; "not special legislation,

but centuries of time,"[98] he concluded, would be required to erase color prejudice.

"The Next Great Question"—black emancipation having been nominally achieved—was advanced by Higginson and other New England reformers in 1868 in the *Independent:* "Why, woman's suffrage to be sure. The case stands next on the docket." For Higginson, the women's cause was an opportunity to redeem one's manhood: "let those of us who had the luck to be born ultraists and men of the future stick to our function."[99]

But radical feminism in the postwar period split on the question of whether blacks should receive the right to vote before it was granted to women. Elizabeth Cady Stanton and Susan B. Anthony opposed the Fifteenth Amendment, as reserved exclusively for the enfranchisement of blacks. When these and other feminists split off from the American Equal Rights Association (to found the National Woman Suffrage Association), Higginson, Lucy Stone, and Mary Livermore created the AWSA periodical *Women's Journal* in order to champion the passage of the Fifteenth Amendment, to defend the family, and to preserve the institution of marriage—then under attack by NWSA free-love advocates like Victoria Woodhull. For fourteen years (1870 - 1884) Higginson coedited and wrote for this journal for women's rights. Later, in 1880, as a member of the Massachusetts Legislature, he cast his ballot for the Woman's Suffrage Bill. Mary Thacher Higginson observed that "certain Irish members, who hated Woman's Suffrage but loved the Colonel, sat outside growling while the vote was taken. They could not bring themselves to vote for the bill, but would not annoy Higginson by voting against it."[100]

During his period in Newport (1864 - 1878), Higginson, like Thoreau, had many lives to lead, and that of the social reformer alternated with that of the writer, for, as he told Emerson, he wished to be "an artist . . . lured by the joy of expression itself."[101] The burden of supporting an invalid wife led him to write essays, short stories, a novel, biographies, and histories, and to lecture widely to a large and admiring public. "To keep up my interest in slavery," he told his old army surgeon, "I am translating Epictetus who is far superior to your dear Antoninus."[102] Epictetus was superior because the philosophy of that Roman slave argued irresistibly the "inevitable laws of retribution"[103] tending toward the restoration of human liberty.

Meanwhile, Higginson began to edit *The Harvard Memorial Biographies* (2 volumes, 1866). Twelve of these brief lives of young Harvard men who had died in the war Higginson wrote himself. In addition, he wrote a series of local-color pieces for the *Atlantic* between 1867 and 1873, gathered under the title *Oldport Days* (1873)—a work much in the vein of Harriet Beecher Stowe's *Oldtown Folks* (1869). His editing of the Harvard biographies and his correspondence with messmates kept the old army days alive to him. After the funeral of one of his army friends, Higginson reflected: "How like a dream it all seems. . . . That I was in it myself seems the dreamiest thing of all; I cannot put my hand upon it in the least, and if someone convinced me, in five minutes some morning, that I never was there at all, it seems as if it would all drop quietly out of my life, and I should read my own letters and think they were someone's else. This is one thing that makes it hard for me to . . . write anything about those days, though sooner or later I should do it."[104]

Later he did—in *Army Life in a Black Regiment* (1870), one of the most intriguing documents of Civil War literature, a work that Howard Mumford Jones has called a "forgotten masterpiece."[105] Afterward, when Higginson reread *Army Life*, he was seized with surprise and interest and "with a sort of despair at the comparative emptiness of all other life after that." He felt that "those times are ever fresh and were perhaps the flower of our lives."[106] Despite his work on *The Harvard Memorial Biographies* and *Army Life*, Higginson felt "an intense longing" to work on his novel. Acknowledging the influence of Hawthorne, he said that he knew "that this Romance (Malbone) is in me like the statue in the marble, for every little while I catch glimpses of parts of it here and there. I have rather held back from it, but a power within steadily forces me on; the characters are steadily forming themselves more and more . . . and it is so attractive to me that were it to be my ruin in fame and fortune I should still wish to keep on."[107] When *Malbone: An Oldport Romance* (1870) was finished, he said that "it is impossible for me to tell what will be thought of this book. I only know that I have enjoyed it more than anything I ever wrote (though writing under great disadvantages) and that the characters are like men and women to me, though not one of them was, strictly speaking, imitated from life, as a whole."[108] Unable to perceive its faults, he was disappointed at the reviewers' criticism, but he expressed satisfaction in the public's "quiet approbation" of the book.

One of his literary projects in the Newport period was *The Intellectual History of Woman*—"my *magnum opus,* if I can really ever get to it." [109] Unfortunately, he never finished this work. Instead, he turned to juvenile history, preparing the *Young Folks' History of the United States* (1875), *English Statesmen* (1875), and *A Book of American Explorers* (1877). Howard W. Hintz is accurate in saying that Higginson's histories (to these we may add his *Larger History of the United States* [1885], *English History for American Readers* [1893] and *Reader's History of American Literature* [1903]) "made no original scholarly contribution." But it is only a forgivable exaggeration to say, as Hintz does, that he was "among the first of American writers to humanize and popularize historical study," or that he "helped materially to lift it out of its ponderous, academic and cataloguing stage, and to inject life, color, dramatic interest, and stylistic grace into historical writing." [110]

Meanwhile, there was some talk of Higginson's becoming president of Harvard, which came to nothing, but he was actually offered the chancellorship of the University of Nebraska, an appointment he declined. The colonel's popularity in the West equaled that in the East, and as a lecturer he was in great demand, for his oratory was legendary, and he drew auditors from great distances. In 1867 he wrote "The remotest places I liked best; it was so strange to dip down on these little Western towns and find an audience all ready and always readers of the 'Atlantic' so glad to see me. One man, an original subscriber to the 'Atlantic Monthly,' brought his family 20 miles to hear me." [111] Howells, in *A Chance Acquaintance,* expressed the West's affection for the "humanitarian preeminence" of Boston, in celebrating it as the home "of the author of the 'Biglow Papers,' of Senator Sumner, of Mr. Whittier, of Dr. Howe, of Colonel Higginson, and of Mr. Garrison." [112]

While Higginson was immensely productive during the immediate postwar years, his life with Mary became an increasing ordeal, owing to her poor health. It was a blow to him that they had never had children, and, as he observed in his journal, "This season [winter] always gives some feeling of loneliness to one of my temperament who is childless . . . and whose home is a hospital and who sees the only object of his care in tears of suffering daily." Nevertheless, though "literary sympathy or encouragement" came slowly, he experienced "an enriching of the mind" that winter, "more ideality, more constructive and creative faculty. . . ." Even so, he felt "haunted with the feeling that it is too soon for any ideal treatment in America. Who reads 'Twice-Told Tales'?"[113]

During the early 1870s, while Higginson was in financial distress, George B. Emerson, a Boston educator, proposed that the colonel write a book on juvenile history for young people. When *Young Folks' History of the United States* was eventually published, to great applause and with extensive sales, Emerson wrote Higginson that he had been "sufficiently repaid" for the advance on the book and would not deduct it from royalties. Higginson remarked: "This munificence gives me $1000 additional in August—probably $2000 in all. For the first time, I think, I begin really to believe that I am to have some money to spend—after fifty years of care and economy." Yet within three months, his publisher, Lee and Shepard, failed, and Higginson's wealth evaporated. Mary's chronic illness and the failure of his publisher weighed him down with anxiety, making it almost impossible for him to write: "The walls seem only to draw closer round me year by year."[114]

XIII   *Return to Cambridge*

In September, 1877, Mary Higginson died, after a week's illness, of "intestinal fever." "She did not suffer much," Higginson wrote a friend, "and closed her courageous life quietly. You are one of those whose personal experience has taught you what it is to lose an object of *care;* how little there seems left to be done, how strange and almost unwelcome the freedom."[115] But within six months after Mary's death, Higginson returned to Cambridge and married Mary Thacher, a niece of Longfellow's first wife. Though he was fifty-five and she only thirty-three, theirs was a complete marital and spiritual bond. Moreover, in January 1880, Minnie, as she was called, gave birth to a daughter, Louisa, a most joyous gift to the childless man. "May I be worthy of the wonderful moment when I first looked round and saw the face of my child," Higginson noted in his journal. "How trivial seem all personal aims and ambitions beside the fact that I am at last the father of a child. Should she die tomorrow she will still be my child somewhere. But she will not die." Within a few weeks, however, the infant Louisa contracted meningitis and died within twenty-four hours. "Thus ends our pride and our earthly hope."[116]

This sorrow was not to be permanent, however, for in July 1881, Minnie presented Wentworth with a second daughter, Margaret Waldo. The light of his life, Margaret learned from him the joy of books and nature. To a friend he remarked, "I have always hoped that if I might not live to see her grow up, I might at least fix myself so definitely in her memory that I should always be a vivid and tender recollection and of this I now for the first time feel sure." In fact he lived to present her to six hundred guests at a coming-out party at Brattle Hall, to see her marriage in 1905 to a Boston physician, and to have the joy of two grandchildren, Wentworth Higginson Barney and Margaret Dellinger Barney. "I have a living representative in the new generation after I am gone," he wrote. They made "immortality seem nearer and less improbable."[117]

In his early years with Minnie on Buckingham Street in Cambridge, Higginson supported his family by writing *Atlantic* articles, reviewing poetry for the *Nation,* and writing biographies and histories. Among the major works of this period are *Short Studies of American Authors* (1880), *Common Sense About Women* (1881), *Margaret Fuller Ossoli* (1884), *Larger History of the United States* (1885), *Hints on Writing and Speech-making* (1887), *Travelers and Outlaws* (1889), and *Life and Times of Francis Higginson* (1890), the latter a biography of his Puritan clerical ancestor.

XIV Practical Politics

Throughout the late 1870s and 1880s, politics and literature continued to dispute for primacy in Higginson's attention. In 1879, he stood for the Massachusetts Legislature as a Republican. During two terms in office, he revealed himself to be a curious amalgam of conservative and liberal thought. Civil service reform and women's rights were the issues that most preoccupied him. He was so appalled by corruption in the civil service that he urged feminists to delay their campaign for equal rights and to work primarily for civil service reform, so that when women *were* granted the right to vote their franchise would not be nullified by corruption in machine politics.

His opposition to the Democratic party's nomination of Benjamin Butler, who stood for equal rights for women, angered leaders in the women's movement and brought him under public attack by such activists as Fanny Garrison Villard, who charged him with a retrogressive "latter-day conservatism." "Personal freedom," he countered, "is an absolute right," while "suffrage is a relative right, belonging to a certain stage of human progress."[118] Ostracized by the women's movement in Massachusetts, he severed his connection, as editor, with the *Woman's Journal,* but he continued to advocate equal rights in women's magazines like *Harper's Bazar* until the end of his life.

Meanwhile, Higginson attacked the anti-Catholic and anti-Semitic sentiment then in Massachusetts, arguing for the rights of religious freedom and opposing any legislation which favored the "tenet of any particular sect of Christians." He disputed the claim that Catholicism was inimical to American political institutions, and attacked the argument for Anglo-Saxon superiority. Finding Catholics, Jews, the Irish, and other ethnic and religious minorities to be supremely worthy of the gifts of American freedom, Higginson was, as Tilden G. Edelstein has remarked, "two decades ahead of his time in advocating the goal of cultural pluralism."[119]

Rejecting the Republican party in the 1880s on the ground that it had become dominated by contractors and speculators, Higginson, as a mugwump, gravitated toward the Democrats. Since suffrage was a relative right, he argued that Southern blacks had probably not been ready for the franchise. Their "lack of interest" in politics suggested that they wisely preferred to pursue education and the acquisition of property in order to elevate their social standing. Higginson now argued that a reconciliation with the South had become essential in the 1880s because radical reconstruction had failed to help the racial situation. Thanks to what his former abolitionist allies called a retrogressive position on Negro rights and labor issues, he received the Democratic nomination for Congress in 1880. Higginson took the position, with respect to the Chicago Haymarket riots, that the arrested laborers were in fact murderers and, as Whittier and Lowell had argued, were well hanged for their crime. Increasingly, he placed strong emphasis on the social responsibility of the business community in the age of the gospel of wealth. The labor movement and the radical antebellum reformers mounted an effective attack on Higginson's puzzling labor and race positions. Frederick Douglass dealt his candidacy the deathblow in accusing him of "having left the Republican Party," of having become a traitor, "not only to that political organization [The Republican Party], but to the cause of liberty itself."[120] Needless to say, Higginson lost the election.

Paradoxically, however, Higginson came to be ideologically allied, in the late 1880s and 1890s, with left-wing progressives who were gravitating toward socialism. Together with Howells, Edward Everett Hale, Julia Ward Howe, and Lucy Stone, Higginson joined the Boston Nationalist Club to advance the nationalization of American industry. Writing in the *Nationalist*, Edward Bellamy's political magazine, Higginson observed: "I have made up my mind that the tendency of events is now toward Nationalism—or State Socialism, if you please—and am prepared to go a few steps further, at any rate, in that direction."[121] He was not in favor of the nationalism of all industries, nor did he think a free-enterprise system to be totally irresponsible. Essentially, Higginson's espousal of state socialism expressed a deeply felt sympathy with the laboring poor and a wish, somehow, to aid in the alleviation of their misery. As Tilden G. Edelstein has remarked, he was opposed to "the awful waste inherent in a system of unchecked competition."[122]

Meanwhile, as American politics became more imperialistic, Higginson deplored the jingoistic imposition of politics and culture on the Spanish colonies in the Caribbean and the Philippines. In Higginson's view, "the American mission was not to conquer distant races," but to aid the Latin American colonies in achieving political self-determination. He urged diplomatic negotiations to resolve the dispute over Cuba in 1898. Fearing American fascination with war as the solution to our differences with Spain, he observed, "war is sweet to those who have never tried it." Arguing that war is "an unnatural and evil thing,"[123] Higginson, together with Mark Twain, William James, Andrew Carnegie, and Carl Schurz, helped to found the Anti-Imperialist League in 1898. "When a nation . . . once enters in the project of managing the affairs of its neighbors it is on the wrong track," he noted. "Freedom is freedom; and it is not for a nation born and reared on this theory to ignore it in judging the affairs of others."[124]

It is worth remarking, moreover, that as the racial situation in the South deteriorated, as Jim Crow legislation, race riots, and lynchings increased, Higginson's racial militancy returned in the last decade of the century. The freedom of black men had always been more important to him than their right to vote. Events in the South forced him to conclude that post-Reconstruction disorders had perhaps *not* been caused by carpetbaggers but by Southerners themselves. Blacks, he argued, "have a right to the freedom of civilization, the freedom of political rights, the freedom not merely to escape being held as slaves, but to have a position as free men that is worth having. The trouble is that the freedom of these people in the South is nominal, not real freedom."[125] Higginson's antiimperialism and his renewed racial militancy had a common basis in his growing opposition to the doctrine of white Anglo-Saxon superiority. In Higginson's view, "an essential part of Democracy" is that "social distinctions should be merely individual, not racial. Character is character and education is education. What social gradations exist," he told William Jennings Bryan, "should be effaced as rapidly as possible."[126]

Yet what was the solution? Siding with Booker T. Washington, he urged an accommodation of blacks to their situation in the South. "I constantly urge my colored friends to be peaceful & hopeful & leave the future to settle matters for itself, under the influence of higher education all around."[127] Higginson's faith that the status of blacks could be elevated principally through equal educational opportunities was rejected by many of the other reformers. In 1909, at the National Negro Conference, sponsored by John Dewey, Jane Addams, Howells, Oswald Garrison Villard, and W. E. B. DuBois, the delegates repudiated Booker T. Washington's faith in patience and proposed a more militant position on civil rights.

Higginson, eighty-five at this time, was unable to attend the conference. But he remarked in an article in the Boston *Evening Transcript* that he had always "regarded the indiscriminate extension of the suffrage to an entire class as class, whether negroes or others, to be politically inexpedient; that is not conducive to the general interest, which in this particular is more important than the interest of the individual." Although he had supported the right of blacks to vote during the Reconstruction era, Higginson's final position was that the enfranchisement of the black had created "great friction between the races and an injury to the negro himself. He would better turn himself to his industrial and educational development than to strive for the establishment of a civil and political status which . . . can never be effectually attained or if ever, only through a conflict of terrible consequences. . . . No white community will ever consent to the political supremacy of either the black man or the colored man or the yellow man. I make this declaration philosophically and as a result of observation and reflection and absolutely without feeling of prejudice, for I have none."[128]

While Higginson's final position is conservative, it is not incomprehensible. Radical militancy has resulted, in the post - World War II period, in greater gains for blacks, but these gains are indirectly the consequence of a temporary strategy of peaceful accommodation and higher education that created the conditions under which positive change has occurred.

XV   *Last Years*

That Higginson should have continued to engage in these public issues of great moment was a testament to his vigor and to his continuous social commitment, even into advanced old age. Yet foremost he was a man of letters who produced in his later years the biographies *Henry Wadsworth Longfellow* (1902), *John Greenleaf Whittier* (1902), and many collections of essays, like *Book and Heart* (1897), and *Carlyle's Laugh and Other Surprises* (1909). Perhaps his chief contribution to American literature was his "discovery" of Emily Dickinson in the 1860s, and his attempt to encourage her and to draw her out of her curious seclusion. Until her death in 1886 they corresponded irregularly. She sent him more than one hundred unpublished poems which, together with others, he and Mabel Loomis Todd edited in two volumes in 1890 and 1891. This eccentric woman, whom Mary called his "cracked poetess," struck him as "a wholly new and original poetic genius" who evaded his analysis and whose metrical and rhyming oddity led him, as her editor, to "smooth" some of her roughnesses. Though Higginson was baffled by her elliptic genius, and erred in regularizing her verses for a genteel American audience, his willingness to engage in her clever epistolary word-games and to play the helpless role of her "preceptor" encouraged her to write that letter to the world which he and Mrs. Todd were eventually to publish.

In a tribute to his career as minister, reformer, and man of letters, Harvard awarded him an honorary LL.D. degree in 1898. And in 1906, as the oldest graduate, Higginson led the Phi Beta Kappa procession at the Harvard commencement, where the audience heard a black graduate address them on "Colonel Higginson and the First Colored Regiment." He outlived most of his antebellum contemporaries, and failed to see fulfilled all of his political and social dreams. Yet in espousing the causes of international arbitration, civil-service reform, free trade, the equalization of the sexes, state socialism, and absolute religious freedom, and in infusing them with the intensity of an absolute moral commitment, Higginson came to be one of the most beloved survivors of the Brahmin tradition. When he died, at the age of eighty-seven in 1911, Higginson was everywhere celebrated as a soldier, critic, writer, and reformer of national stature. At his funeral in Cambridge, he was given the rites of a military burial; it was conducted by the Thomas Wentworth Higginson Loyal Legion Post, assisted by a detachment of black soldiers. The flag of the First South Carolina Volunteers was spread over the coffin. His poems "Waiting for the Bugle" and "To Thine Eternal Arms, Oh God" were sung. His fitting epitaph would have been these favorite lines from Walt Whitman:

> Joy, Shipmate, joy!
> (Pleas'd to my soul at death I cry)
> Our life is closed, our life begins
> The long, long anchorage we leave,
> The ship is clear at last, she leaps,
> She swiftly courses from the shore,
>   Joy, Shipmate, joy!

CHAPTER 2

First Principles of a Man of Letters

TO understand the work of Thomas Wentworth Higginson—
whether his subject is history, biography, military life, or
imaginative literature—it is important to understand the premises
of his thought, the first principles of his intellectual and moral life.
Only by grasping the underlying orientation to all of his literary efforts can we perceive the consistency of analysis in his books and
understand the sometimes idiosyncratic, sometimes remarkably
acute, conclusions to which he came.

I have already remarked in the preceding biographical overview
that T. W. Higginson was in his youth a vocal apostle of the
"Newness," that indigenous mode of Transcendentalism that
developed in New England in the 1830s. The "Newness" gave
Higginson a spiritual and ethical base from which he was able to
move out, in various directions, through the Sisterhood of Reforms
and into the literary life. Chief among the characteristics of
Transcendentalism was a belief in an Unseen Power making for
righteousness in the world. Opposed to the doctrines of Calvinism
and to the necessity of a church liturgy of formal observances,
Higginson believed in the soul's capacity to form a direct union
with the Unseen Power, or God, through openness to one's intuition
of the true and the good. The conventional churches in New
England were too formalistic and negative, for him, in their
emphasis on dogma. Even Unitarianism, which offered a less doc-
trinaire, non-Trinitarian fellowship, based on the brotherhood of all
men, was for Higginson unduly formalistic, as we have seen.
Higginson therefore preferred to minister to nondenominational
ethical societies like those at Newburyport and Worcester.

I   *Higginson's Creed*

The ethical and religious creed which underlay all of Higginson's
reform activism and his literary work is best defined in his essays

"The Sympathy of Religions" and "Philanthropy," both published in *Studies in History and Letters*, and in a sermon entitled "My Creed," written in the 1860s, about the time of the foundation of the Free Religious Association of Boston, of which Higginson was elected president.

In "The Sympathy of Religions," Higginson argued that "our true religious life begins when we discover that there is an Inner Light, not infallible but invaluable, which 'lighteth every man that cometh into the world.' "[1] This inner light, for Higginson, was "something to steer by," a guide through the vicissitudes of existence. Thus he placed great emphasis on the Self, or self-reliance, as a key to understanding truth. Yet Higginson was no Quaker, inasmuch as he believed that the "great historic religions of the world," however shackled by doctrines, were yet "full of life and activity. All over the world the Divine influence moves men," he observed. "There is a sympathy in religions, and this sympathy is shown alike in their origin, their records, and their career" (318 - 19). In this essay Higginson argued that the "new knowledge of the religions of the world" only testified to the "sympathy" among them: "They all show similar aims, symbols, forms, weaknesses, and aspirations." As he analyzed the common features of the great historic religions, Higginson observed that "under many forms there is but one religion, whose essential creed is the Fatherhood of God and the Brotherhood of man,—disguised by corruptions, symbolized by mythologies, ennobled by virtues, degraded by vices, but still the same" (320).

Higginson adduced extensive evidence, from classical times forward, to document the view that though the names may differ, there is but one God, one source of religion. Zoroastrianism, Christianity, Buddhism, and Mohammedanism were all, for him, evidences of Natural Religion plus an individual name, that of the founder. In all religions, he encountered "the same great doctrines, good or bad,—regeneration, predestination, atonement, the future life, the final judgment, the Divine Reason or Logos, and the Trinity." The same religious devotees recurred in them all—monks, missionaries, priests, and pilgrims. The same rituals were performed—prayers, liturgies, sacrifices, sermons, hymns. The same implements were employed—frankincense, candles, holy water, relics, amulets, votive offerings. The same symbols were held up —the cross, the ball, the triangle, the serpent, the all-seeing eye, the halo of rays, the tree of life. They all had similar saints, angels, and martyrs. "The same holiness attached to particular cities, rivers, and mountains. The same prophecies and miracles,—the dead restored and evil spirits cast out" (324 - 25).

Consequently, Higginson asserted his belief "that all religion is natural, all revealed." All religions recognized the conception of a creator, the notion of immortality, and charity or brotherly love. The forgiveness of injuries, the love of enemies, the overcoming of evil with good—all of these virtues Higginson found recorded in the sacred scriptures of the great religions, Eastern and Western. The one unpardonable sin, for Higginson, was exclusiveness. He believed that there was "not a single maxim, or idea, or application, or triumph, that any one religion can claim as exclusively its own. Neither faith, nor love, nor truth, nor disinterestedness, nor forgiveness, nor patience, nor peace, nor equality, nor education, nor missionary effort, nor prayer, nor honesty, nor the sentiment of brotherhood, nor reverence for woman, nor the spirit of humility, nor the fact of martyrdom, nor any other good thing, is monopolized by any form of faith" (346).

Given the basic identity of the religious impulse and the mere accident of its external forms, "What faith in humanity springs up, what trust in God, when one recognizes the sympathy of religions!" (328). This faith in humanity thus led him to "the idea of Incarnation," the Divine Man. Even with regard to this doctrine, Higginson argued that "all religions sympathize, and, with slight modifications, each is a copy of the other." For Higginson, Jesus was just a man, albeit that religious spirit who stood at the head of the human procession. And he quoted with approval the saying of the Platonic philosopher Porphyry that "that noble soul [Jesus], who had ascended into heaven, has by a certain fatality become an occasion of error" (327). The truth for Higginson was that all men are divine and worthy of respect and love.

Though Higginson believed that Christianity stood "highest in its moral results," he yet saw that Christendom had accommodated itself to slavery and that maltreatment of the Indians constituted a like moral failing in the history of this religion. He observed that "when we fully comprehend the sympathy of religions we shall deal with other faiths on fairer terms. We shall cease trying to free men from one superstition by inviting them into another. The true missionaries are men inside each religion who have outgrown its limitations" (354).

Higginson's essay "Philanthropy" is principally a review of the origin of the term, in Greece, and the transmission of the concept through Roman times into the nineteenth century. The significance of the essay, however, as an index of Higginson's ethical position, from which all of the reform activities were launched, is contained in the saying of Cicero—that "we are framed by Nature to love mankind; this is the foundation of the law"—and the maxim of Quintilian, who wrote that we should "give heed to a stranger in the name of the universal brotherhood which binds together all men under the common father of Nature" (374).

In "My Creed," Higginson emphasized the unarguable reality of the moment of intuition, when God (or call it what you will) manifests his presence. This divine power came as a supplementing strength in moments of "care, sorrow, depression, perplexity when neither study nor action nor friends will clear the horizon."[2] The advent of this "Unseen Power" he felt to be independent of church tradition or the mythology of belief: "It may be in a church; it may equally well be in a solitary room or on a mountain height." In any event, this experience of the intersection of the divine and the human Higginson called (in the language of the mystics) "the flight of the Alone, to the Alone." For him, this experience—"call it prayer or reverie or what you please—is as substantial as anything else that can come to us."

II   Science and Mysticism

Higginson did not believe that the new empirical science—as represented by Darwin, Huxley, and Spencer—threatened a belief in such moments of divine or mystical perception. "All honor to the great scientific investigations which are to so many the only path out of crushing opposition," he wrote, "but let us recognize also that science is not all, and that help and strength may still come from a region unexplored by science." The mystical experience might be "unsystematic, unmeasured, occasional," but for Higginson the reality of the transcendental experience of the benignant Unseen Power elevated the soul, and "it is something to know what that level is."

Higginson did not believe that the mystical experience of joy was essential to the moral life. Indeed, he knew many devout, virtuous, and heroic reformers whose self-abnegation was marked by the renunciation of all joy. But Higginson was not one of them. He did not believe in "a great deal of gray work . . . done by heroic men in a spirit so grim and determined that if it does not fatigue the world for which it is applied, it wears out the man who applies it." Instead, he believed in the experience of personal religion, in the old sense, but "purified from other repulsive associations of cant and hypocrisy." Rather than renunciation and self-abnegation, in a grim, humorless spirit, life "should attain to peace and joy."

Higginson was not, in my view, a mystic. His diaries, journals, correspondence, and publications record no experience directly expressive of the mystical state, as defined by his contemporary William James, for instance, or Evelyn Underhill in *Mysticism*. Yet the sense of peace and joy which characterized Higginson's sunny temperament derived from a sublime faith in the existence of a God who manifests himself directly to man; in the order and meaning of the universe and human experience; in the brotherhood of all men; in the unity of all religions; in the necessity of self-development; and in vigorous social activism intended to realize justice in human society at large. Higginson knew that the struggle to perfect the self, and society, would be marked by many preliminary defeats. But with faith and will all things are possible. "I know that the sunny heart and the healthy body can gain out of pain and bereavement and sin and privation and nursing only a renewed faith in the eternal law. I know that all which is noblest is immortal."[3]

III   *Spiritual and Physical Development*

As to his sunny heart, or soul, Higginson felt that he must develop himself spiritually in order to preach the truth and to become a great leader and teacher of men. But his education was not merely that of the intellect; he undertook spiritual exercises, affirming the principles of virtue and constantly refining his ethical perceptions and testing himself by acting on his principles. Since the body was the temple of the Holy Spirit, it goes without saying that he was a man of pure habits. He neither smoked nor drank and, indeed, he preached tirelessly in behalf of temperance, chastity, and personal morality. Higginson also developed his body. He loved boyhood athletics as a matter of course. But in later life he became an avid physical-culture enthusiast. His first essay for the new *Atlantic* magazine was "Saints and Their Bodies" (1858). Distressed at the "declining state of physical fitness among American men and women,"[4] Higginson recommended and engaged in ice-skating, swimming, walking, riding, boating, and all other kinds of physical sports. Recuperating in Newport, after his Civil War injury, he exercised regularly in a local gymnasium with barbells, the parallel bars, the horse, and flying rings. His diaries are studded with entries like these: "In gymnasium climbed rope to top with arms only. I know no other man of fifty who is so good in gymnasium"; "Afternoon—parallel bars a few times. It was astonishing how much they did for me"; and "Best gymnasium afternoon I have ever had, best condition,—forward & back somersaults in bars several times—hung by bent right arm, . . . circled bar without spring, . . . felt no fatigue & wished to keep on beyond an hour."[5] Higginson created athletic teams, conducted group calisthenic exercises, and propagandized tirelessly for physical education as a requirement in the schools, especially for young American girls, who seemed to him subject to nervous disabilities because of their physical condition.

"Saints and Their Bodies," "Gymnastics," and "The Health of Our Girls"—all reprinted in *Out-Door Papers* (1886)—give full and rich testimony to the value, for the life of the mind and spirit, of a well-developed physical body. One of Higginson's female acquaintances in Worcester wrote to a friend in 1859: "What do you say to nineteen cars being loaded with twelve hundred men, women, boys, and girls, all bound for the ice, equipped with skates, hand-sleds, and the like? . . . Mr. Higginson's articles in the *Atlantic*, 'Saints and Their Bodies,' 'Physical Training,' and his lectures and personal efforts seem to have stimulated everybody, old and young, grave and gay, to participate in this excellent and fascinating exercise. Last winter some rigid-minded people called it 'Higginson's Revival.' This winter he marvels at the excellent skaters among the ladies, and declares they must have learned last summer."[6] Higginson's whole life was thus a repudiation of the error that "physical vigor and spiritual sanctity are incompatible."[7]

IV *Stoic Emphases*

In view of Higginson's strenuous lifelong program of physical conditioning, the serenity with which he bore the rigors of his military service, and the uncomplaining ordeal of nursing his wife Mary through her permanent invalidism, it is no exaggeration to say that Higginson's personal philosophy was strongly influenced by the principles of stoicism. When he translated the works of Epictetus, he expressed admiration for the practical value of

Epictetus's philosophy, in contrast to "those cloudy regions of Proclus and Plotinus. . . . " In addition, he defended stoicism against some of the Christian criticisms of that philosophy, absolving it of arrogance, coldness, and tolerance of suicide. He translated Epictetus at the conclusion of the Civil War, and saw a singular appropriateness "in coming to this work from a camp of colored soldiers, whose great exemplar Toussaint l'Ouverture, made the works of this his fellow slave a favorite manual." Of Epictetus he wrote: "I am acquainted with no book more replete with high conceptions of the Deity, and noble aims for man; nor do I know any in which the inevitable laws of retribution are more grandly stated. . . . " In the preface to this translation, Higginson expressed satisfaction in calling "anew the public attention to those eternal principles on which alone true prosperity is based; and, in a period of increasing religious toleration, to revive the voice of one who bore witness to the highest spiritual truths, ere the present sects were born."[8]

Out of the views expressed in his creed and in "The Sympathy of Religions" derived his belief in the brotherhood of man, his love of philanthropy, and his hatred of slavery as a violation of human equality before God. From such beliefs also sprang his moral indignation at the legal and cultural subordination of women. His condemnation of materialism and his liberal labor views, his sympathy with immigrants and oppressed minorities like Catholics and Jews, his opposition to political imperialism, and his quasi-socialistic political views all derived from these first principles of religious and ethical belief. These beliefs, however, required Higginson to act, to be at the center of dissent and political activism—first as an abolitionist, preaching and even leading the mob to free an escaped slave; then as a woman's suffrage militant with Lucy Stone, Elizabeth Cady Stanton, and Susan B. Anthony; as a temperance crusader; and as a frequent candidate (and an elected Massachusetts legislator) battling in behalf of all uncompleted reforms. And out of these beliefs grew his passion for a democratic American literature—of, by, and for the people, reflecting American themes, the American character, and American values.

V   *The "Curse" of Versatility*

It is as a writer that Higginson can now best be known. He was not a great writer, for he turned his energies to so many different tasks that he excelled in perhaps none of them. Howard Mumford Jones has even argued that "he was . . . the victim of a liberal education," in that Harvard—with its new elective system—"never taught him what to write about." And in the era of the Newness, "the value system" of the young Transcendentalists prevented them "from following any particular occupation"—lest they warp the soul or "do violence to the 'ideal.' "[9]

Higginson himself eventually came to understand his personal limitation. "The trouble with me," he once wrote, "is too great a range of tastes and interests. I love to do everything, to study everything, to contemplate and to write. I was never happier than when in the army entirely absorbed in active duty; yet I love literature next—indeed almost better; and I need either two lives or forty-eight hours in the day to do it all."[10] The diffusion of his talents and energies thus kept Higginson from being superlative in any one of his elected areas of performance. Still, his published works constitute a highly readable and enjoyable compendium of nineteenth-century liberal aspirations. He wrote and edited more than thirty-five books and published hundreds of periodical articles. And—though "cursed with versatility"[11]—he produced at least two masterpieces, now well-nigh forgotten—*Army Life in a Black Regiment* and *Cheerful Yesterdays*. With this understanding of his first principles, let us now turn to his most important published works.

CHAPTER 3

The Emancipation of Blacks:
Army Life in a Black Regiment

THROUGHOUT the 1840s and 1850s, while the abolition movement was building, Wentworth Higginson was absorbing the strange enthusiasm of antislavery reformers like Garrison, Phillips, Lucy Stone, Mrs. Child, the Grimké sisters, Theodore Parker, and Samuel Gridley Howe. Emerson had said that "the Abolitionists should resist, because they are literalists; they know exactly what they object to, and there is a government possible which will content them."[1] Some abolitionists held to the necessity of participating in the electoral process, in order to change the law; Higginson advocated disunion and secession from a national government unwilling to abolish slavery. As Higginson reflected on the matter, he wrote to a friend that "the great reason why the real apostles of truth don't make any more impression is this—the moment any person among us begins to broach any 'new views' and intimate that all things aren't exactly right, the conservatives lose no time in holding up their fingers and branding him as an unsafe person—fanatic, visionary, insane, and all the rest of it. . . ." This, he felt, had rightly been the case with all reforms, since "it is the enthusiastic (i.e. half-cracked people) who begin all reforms." Mrs. Child, he observed, "has long been proscribed as an entirely unsafe person and as for Mr. Emerson and Mr. Alcott, it doesn't do for a sober person even to *think* of them."[2]

So vocal was he, in his opposition to slavery, that the conservatives called him "swart-minded Higginson" and accused him of substituting his private opinions for the law. But he pointed to a Higher Law, the law of human freedom, which would be served, even perhaps, unfortunately, through the instrumentality of violence. That violence eventually erupted at Fort Sumter, South Carolina, in 1861. And out of the war, and his service in it, came one of Higginson's major books, *Army Life in a Black Regiment*.

59

Army Life in a Black Regiment (1870) is an account of Higginson's comand, between 1862 and 1864, of the first regiment of freed slaves in the United States Army. After it had become clear that the emancipation of the slaves was an actual intention of the federal government in waging the war, Higginson raised a regiment of Massachusetts volunteers in early 1862. Hardly had he begun to train his men, however, when he received a surprising invitation from General Rufus Saxton to take command of the First South Carolina Volunteers. Higginson was not a trained officer: he had never administered an organization of the kind; and, as a minister, he was hardly prepared by his vocation for leading troops, of any color, in combat. Nevertheless, it is a tribute to the foresight of Lincoln's military command that this radical abolitionist and spokesman for racial equality should have been selected to command a most important enterprise for the freedmen.

His self-confidence, however, was based on his prophetic knowledge that war would come. Since "the Kansas troubles," his mind "had dwelt on military matters more or less during all that time." He felt that the best volunteer regiments "already exhibited a high standard of drill and discipline," and that the freed slaves could be brought tolerably near that standard. He had "perfect confidence" that they could be effectively trained since he knew, "by experience, the qualities of their race," and knew that they had "home and household and freedom to fight for. . . ."[3]

But suspicious that he might be slated to head "a mere plantation guard or a day-school in uniform" (3), Higginson went to South Carolina to estimate the possibilities of this appointment. On arriving in Beaufort, he was ushered into "an old plantation, with stately magnolia avenue, decaying house, and tiny church amid the woods, reminding me of Virginia; behind it stood a neat encampment of white tents, 'And there,' said my companion, 'is your future regiment' " (9). From "the broken windows of this forlorn plantation house" Higginson could look down the "avenues of great live-oaks, with their hard shining leaves, and their branches hung with a universal drapery of soft, long moss, like fringe trees stuck with grayness." Beyond was "the sandy soil, scantly covered with coarse grass" bristling "with sharp palmettoes and aloes." He found all the vegetation to be "stiff, shining, semi-tropical, with nothing soft or delicate in its texture. Numerous plantation buildings totter around, all slovenly and unattractive," he observed, "while the interspaces are filled with all manner of wreck and refuse, pigs, fowls, dogs, and omnipresent Ethiopian infancy. All this," he was later to say, is "the universal Southern panorama . . ." (11).

After reviewing the sea-island camp and the men, Higginson accepted the assignment. Facing him was the task of transforming eight hundred newly freed slaves into disciplined combat soldiers. *Army Life in a Black Regiment* is the fascinating record of his command of this regiment—the drill and disciplining of these men and the nature of their life in camp (including their rituals and folk songs, their religious sentiments, and their relationships among themselves and with whites). The book recounts his regiment's picket duties; its expeditions up the St. Marys, the St. Johns, and the Edisto rivers; its forays into the Southern interior to collect supplies; its invasion and occupation of Jacksonville, Florida; the Rebel ambush in which he was wounded; and his subsequent medical discharge and departure from the South.

Much of the book is written in the form of a diary, since Higginson felt that journal entries gave freshness and immediacy to the experience narrated. The sections of the book that deal with combat experiences, however, are retrospective narrations, since Higginson was naturally unable to keep notes while in the field. In 1884, Higginson added a final chapter analyzing his impressions of the experience after a fourteen-year interval.

I   *The Colonel under Fire*

The energy, zeal, and daring of the black troops were put to the test in one of the regiment's first expeditions, up the St. Marys River, in search of lumber and slaves on the interior plantations. Higginson and his ship patrol undertook a nocturnal ascent of "an unknown river" deep into the "enemy's country, where one glides in the dim moonlight between dark hills and meadows, each turn of the channel making it seem like an inland lake, and cutting you off as by a barrier from all behind,—with no sign of human life, but an occasional picket fire left glimmering beneath the bank, or the yelp of a dog from some low-lying plantation" (112 - 13). The strategy of the Confederate cavalry and the partisans was to let the federal patrol ascend the river and ambush them on their return down water. Near Reed's Bluff and Scrubby Bluff, the patrol came under Rebel fire. Most of the black soldiers had been ordered below. "My men were pretty well now imprisoned below in the hot and crowded hold, and actually fought each other, the officers afterward said, for places at the open port-holes, from which to aim. Others implored Higginson to land them, exclaiming that they 'supposed de Cunnel knew best,' but it was 'mighty mean' to be shut up down below, when they might be 'fightin' de Secesh *in de clar field*' " (124 - 25). Higginson's patrol boat successfully ran this gauntlet. Though the expedition was a slight one, accounts of it in the newspapers occupied a great deal of space, "so intense was the interest which then attached to the novel experiment of employing black troops" (128). Such was the uncertainty of war correspondence that, after one of these upriver expeditions, it was reported in the Northern press that Higginson and his troops "had been captured and shot." Indeed, Higginson "had afterwards the pleasure of reading my own obituary in a Northern Democratic journal . . ." (163).

In the camp, the memory of the raid up the St. Marys "was preserved . . . by many legends of adventure,—growing vaster and more incredible as time wore on,—and by morning appeals to the surgeon of some veteran invalids, who could now cut off all reproofs and suspicions with 'Doctor, I's been a sickly pusson eber since de *expeditious*' " (129 - 30).

II   *The Invasion of Jacksonville*

The success of the expedition up the St. Marys encouraged the Department of the South, early in 1863, to experiment further along the same line. It was proposed in Washington that Colonel Higginson's regiment undertake the invasion of Jacksonville, Florida, on the St. Johns River. Jacksonville had already been twice taken and twice evacuated by federal troops. "The present proposition was, to take and hold it with a brigade of less than a thousand men, carrying, however, arms and uniforms for twice that number, and a month's ration" (133). In a letter to the Secretary of War, dated March 14, 1863, General Saxton observed that "the object of this expedition . . . to occupy Jacksonville" was to "make it the base of operations for the arming of negroes, and securing in this way possession of the entire State of Florida." General Saxton believed that nothing could cause "greater panic throughout the whole Southern coast" than a "raid of the colored troops in Florida." The wisdom of his order was confirmed by the dismay of General Joseph Finnegan of the Confederate States Army, who reported to his superiors that the invasion would lead to "intercourse . . . between negroes on the plantations and those in the enemy's service." This infiltration, "conducted through swamps and under cover of night, . . . cannot be prevented. A few weeks will suffice to corrupt the entire slave population of east Florida" (176 - 77).

Higginson was delighted with this plan, since his men needed action in order to prove their reliability as combat soldiers. "The main objects of your expedition," General Saxton told him, "are to carry the proclamation of freedom to the enslaved; to call all loyal men into the service of the United States; to occupy as much of the State of Florida as possible with the forces under your command; and to neglect no means consistent with the usages of civilized warfare to weaken, harass, and annoy those who are in rebellion against the Government of the United States" (135 - 36). Embarking on the *John Adams*, the *Boston*, the *Burnside*, and the *Uncas*, Higginson and his troops sailed by night to Fernandina and rendezvoused near the harbor of Jacksonville. "It was 8 o'clock. We were now directly opposite the town; yet no sign of danger was seen; not a rifle shot was heard; not a shell rose hissing in the air. The *Uncas* rounded to, and dropped anchor in the stream; by previous agreement, I steamed to an upper pier of the town, Colonel Montgomery to a lower one; the little boat-howitzers were run out upon the wharfs, and presently to the angles of the chief streets; and the pretty town was ours without a shot. In spite of our detention, the surprise had been complete, and not a soul in Jacksonville had dreamed of our coming" (142 - 43). So unexpected was the invasion of this expeditionary force that the Confederate forces were totally unprepared and Jacksonville was taken without even a shot. Higginson set up temporary headquarters and thus imposed federal control on the only post on the mainland in the Department of the South.

The capture of Jacksonville, however, produced its difficulties. The chief of these was the virtually impossible task of holding it with merely nine hundred men. To deceive the enemy, Higginson deployed troops throughout the town, set up empty tents in many quarters, moved the units back and forth in the harbor in order to conceal the size of his troop, and ordered white reinforcements. Meanwhile, he faced the difficult problem of disciplining some black soldiers, originally from Florida, who now had their former masters at their mercy. They were surprisingly free from revengefulness, even though they fought under the sentence of death, for a Confederate order "consigned the new colored troops and their officers to a felon's death if captured . . . 'Dere's no flags ob truce for us,' the men would contemptuously say. 'When de

Secesh fight de *Fus' Souf* (First South Carolina), 'he fight in
earnest' " (206). Higginson also fought with the noose round his
own neck, for an act of the Confederate Congress stipulated that
"every white person being a commissioned officer . . . who, during
the present war, shall command negroes or mulattos in arms against
the Confederate States shall, if captured, be put to death or be
otherwise punished at the discretion of the court" (359n).

Higginson felt that the success of the black regiment depended
on their being treated exactly like other volunteers in the Union army. The soldiers were "constantly kidded by their families and
friends with the prospect of risking their lives in the service and
being paid nothing." They only half-believed that they would
receive "the full pay of soldiers." But "with what utter humiliation
were we, their officers, obliged to confess to them, eighteen months
afterwards, that it was their distrust which was wise, and our faith in
the pledges of the United States Government which was
foolishness! The attempt was made to put them off with half pay"
(21).

When the Union government reduced the pay of black soldiers
by half, Higginson wrote burning letters to senators, congressmen,
abolitionist friends, and Northern newspapers, deploring the
government's refusal to pay the men what they had been promised
at the time of enlistment. The government's position, he told
Senator Sumner, "will be the greatest blow ever struck at successful
emancipation in the Department of the South, for it will destroy all
confidence in the honesty of the government."[4] To the *New York
Times* he wrote "we presume too much on the supposed ignorance
of these men. I have never yet found a man in my regiment so
stupid as not to know when he was cheated. If fraud proceeds from
the government itself, so much the worse, for this strikes at the
foundation of all rectitude, all honor, all obligation."[5] In due
course, Higginson's campaign succeeded; in 1865, Congress
restored full pay to the black troops.

Shortly after the occupation of Jacksonville, the military command issued an inexplicable order for Higginson and his troops to
evacuate the town. The men were crushed and disappointed at this
turn of events. Many of the civilian residents begged to accompany
Higginson and his troops on their evacuation. Their departure was
something of an opera buffa since the townspeople of Jacksonville
"at once developed that insane mania for aged and valueless
trumpery which always seizes upon the human race . . . in

moments of danger" (173). While the colonel was patiently explaining to them that their worthless furniture could not be taken aboard ship, some of the white troops under his command set fire to the town. Though perhaps no more than twenty-five buildings were burned down, the colonel was dismayed, though he was pleased that the Northern press correctly absolved the colored regiment from having had anything to do with this wanton act of barbarism.

Back in South Carolina, Higginson grew restive at the desk in regimental headquarters. Although "restricted by duty from doing many foolish things," one night Higginson decided to collect first-hand intelligence about Confederate outposts on the other side of the river. Riding down to the causeway, he told his black sentries that he intended to go for a swim. Partly to test his powers of physical endurance and partly to satisfy his boyish love of adventure, Higginson slipped into the water and swam across the river to the spot where Rebel pickets were patrolling the shore. Fortunately he was not detected, but on the return trip, much of which he swam under water, he became disoriented when the tide turned. Swept downstream he wound up in the marshes well below his camp. When he eventually emerged from the water, he was accosted by a black sentry from the First South Carolina Volunteers. It is a wonder that he was not shot as a Rebel spy as he stood there (apparently naked). Fortunately he knew the countersign, and the sentry recognized him and presented arms, despite the absence of any visible rank.

III   *Upriver Forays*

Higginson and his troops engaged in none of the "great campaigns, where a man, a regiment, a brigade, is but a pawn in the game" (229). Much of their time was spent in fighting off Rebel irregulars while liberating slaves and foraging for lumber, food, and other supplies. In due course, "these upriver raids reached the dignity of a fine art" (156). Though they were relatively insignificant compared to a Vicksburg or Gettysburg, Higginson found in them "a charm" in the "more free and adventurous life of partisan warfare, where, if total sphere be humbler, yet the individual has more relative importance, as the sense of action is more personal and keen" (227). His adventures with the black troops had "the same elements of picturesqueness" that belonged to the partisan skirmishes of the Revolutionary War. Their expedition up the

Edisto River to destroy a bridge on the Charleston and Savannah Railway was one of these exciting raids. Liberating slaves from the upriver plantations, confiscating bales of cotton, and burning the rice houses in accordance with their orders, Higginson and his troops came under Rebel fire as they descended the river. For the first time Higginson discovered that "there were certain compensating advantages in a slightly built craft, as compared with one more substantial; the missiles never lodged in the vessel, but crashed through some thin partitions as if it were paper, to explode beyond us, or fall harmless in the water. Splintering, the chief source of wounds and death in wooden ships, was entirely avoided; the danger was that our machinery might be disabled, or that shots might strike beyond the water-line and sink us" (246).

In this attack more than fifteen cannonballs and grapeshot passed through the vessel, tearing apart rigging and shattering the pilothouse. Higginson was wounded in this attack by "a sudden blow in the side," as if some prizefighter had doubled him up. Upon examination the wound proved "to have been produced by the grazing of a ball, which, without tearing a garment, had yet made a large part of my side black and blue, leaving a sensation of paralysis which made it difficult to stand." Dazed, he remembered trying to comprehend what had happened to him and was "impressed by an odd feeling that I had now got my share, and should henceforth be a great deal safer than any of the rest" (247). Nevertheless, he and the captain of the ship managed to get the craft and his men back to camp. Higginson declined to go into his "personal record of convalescence," but he was perfectly confident that his "habitual abstinence" from whiskey left "no food for peritoneal inflammation to feed upon" (251).

Convalescing at Camp Shaw, he was impatient to resume active duty and indeed returned too soon, suffering a "complete prostration," compounded perhaps by malarial fever. Higginson underplayed the significance of this wound, but it was serious enough to oblige him to resign his commission, in May 1864, when he was ordered home as an invalid. The expedition in which he was wounded was not a major campaign in the war, but the colonel was later to say that "the day was worth all it cost, and more" (252). Before the war, "the rescue of even one man from slavery" had seemed a truly great thing. Afterward how little seemed "the liberation of two hundred." Yet no one could say in 1864 how the Civil

War might end. Thus the satisfaction he took at the time in the liberation of every single slave.

IV   *The Northern Audience*

Much of *Army Life* is designed to correct Northern misconceptions of the character of Southern blacks. Higginson remarked that "at first, of course, they all looked just alike; the variety comes afterwards, and they are just as distinguishable . . . as so many whites" (13). At the beginning, Higginson regarded blacks as "simple, docile, and affectionate almost to the point of absurdity" (14). Living with them was "a wonderfully strange sensation," for they were "a race affectionate, enthusiastic, grotesque, and dramatic beyond all others" (6). Higginson also found the landscape, the cuisine, and command problems different from anything in his earlier experience. He drilled his regiment by day and inspected their quarters by night, observing that they subsisted on pork and oysters and sweet potatoes and rice and hominy and cornbread and milk, mysterious griddle-cakes of corn and pumpkin, preserves made of pumpkin-chips, and "other fanciful productions of Ethiop art" (29).

Although their servitude had reduced them to a race of "grown-up children," these freed slaves were eager to extend the blessings of liberty to their brothers and sisters on the interior plantations. They constantly sang and exhorted one another, and one took the stump and poignantly proclaimed, "We'll neber desert de ole flag, boys, neber; we hab lib under it for *eighteen hundred sixty-two years,* and we'll die for it now" (31). As Higginson grew more acquainted with the men, the individuality of each emerged, first their faces, then their characters, and he perceived "the desire they show to do their duty, and to improve as soldiers." Higginson noted that they evidently thought a great deal about it, for they felt that "we white men cannot stay and be their leaders always and that they must learn to depend on themselves, or else relapse into their former condition" (43).

Higginson found their "religious spirit" one of the most interesting aspects of these Southern blacks, influencing them in both negative and positive ways. On the negative side, he felt that their religion cultivated in them "the feminine virtues first," making them "patient, meek, resigned" (72 - 73). "Imbued from childhood with the habit of submission," they could endure, he discovered, nearly everything. But he was also pleased to see that their religion strengthened them by conferring on them "zeal, energy, daring" (73). Their religion he took to be "the highest form of mysticism"; and he quoted approvingly the regimental surgeon, who declared that they were all "natural transcendentalists" (73).

V *Black Spirituals*

One of the valuable qualities of *Army Life* is Higginson's record of the Negro spirituals of his troops. As a man of letters he had always been "a faithful student of the Scottish ballads," and he had envied Sir Walter Scott for the delight he took in "tracing them out amid their own heather and of writing them down piece-meal from the lips of aged crones" (269). Set down into "the midst of a kindred world of unwritten songs, as simple and indigenous as the Border Minstrelsy, more uniformly plaintive, almost always more quaint, and often as essentially poetic," Higginson listened to and recorded the texts of thirty-six Negro spirituals. He transcribed them "as nearly as possible, in the original dialect" (271). His transcription is, insofar as one may judge, reasonably accurate. In any event, he tried to make the text easy to read, since he wished to avoid what seemed to him "the only error of Lowell's 'Biglow Papers' in respect to dialect,—the occasional use of an extreme misspelling, which merely confuses the eye without taking us any closer to the pecularity of sound" (271). In general, the spirituals he recorded are typical of others in that they expressed "nothing but patience for this life,—nothing but triumph in the next" (276). Through them the slaves could "sing themselves, as had their fathers before them, out of the contemplation of their own estate, into the sublime scenery of the Apocalypse" (299). Of those recorded, "I Know Moon-Rise" is one of the most moving:

> I know moon-rise, I know star-rise,
>   Lay dis body down.
> I walk in de moonlight, I walk in de starlight,
>   To lay dis body down.
> I'll walk in de graveyard, I'll walk through de graveyard,
>   To lay dis body down.
> I'll lie in de grave and stretch out my arms;
>   Lay dis body down.

> I go to de judgment in de evenin' of de day,
>> When I lay dis body down;
> And my soul and your soul will meet in de day
>> When I lay dis body down.

When we consider that slaves were often jailed for singing songs of freedom anticipated in the next life, because the slavemasters saw them as seditious symbolic statements, the poignance of these lines becomes almost unbearable. There is no doubt that these spirituals were "but the vocal expression of the simplicity of their faith and the sublimity of their long resignation" (300).

Equally fascinating, in view of the contemporary debate over the oral tradition in primitive poetry, was Higginson's curiosity about "whether they had always a conscious and definite origin in some leading mind, or whether they grew by gradual accretion, in an almost unconscious way" (295). Inquiring among those troops who were especially good singers, Higginson extracted the admission from one young man that "some good spirituals . . . are start jest out o' curiosity. I been a-raise a sing myself, once" (296). This remark convinced Higginson that spirituals tend to be invented by a single singer, whose song is picked up by other singers who, perhaps, play variations on the original invention. Thanks to Higginson's work on Negro spirituals, interest developed throughout the nation in the folksongs of the slaves. As Howard N. Meyer has suggested, Higginson "had the immediate distinction of having opened the door to the wider interest" in spirituals "and later the credit—not always assigned to him—of having been the pioneer recorder"[6] of some of the finest of the black folksongs.

VI *The Black as Man and Soldier*

Perhaps the most intriguing chapter in *Army Life in a Black Regiment* is that entitled "The Negro As a Soldier." Higginson had feared that "they might show less fibre, less tough and dogged resistance, than whites, during a prolonged trial,—a long, disastrous march, for instance, or the hopeless defense of a besieged town" (37). But the troops proved without question that they were capable of the discipline, daring, and energy of white combat troops. Moreover, they had been tested under fire and had proved the wisdom of the military command in Washington which had

directed them to invade Jacksonville and to foment insurrection on
the plantations in the interior.

Higginson's fears thus proved groundless. The particular
assignments of his troops, moreover, proved to be "an especially
favorable test" of their capacities. "They had more to fight for than
the whites. Besides the flag and the Union, they had home and wife
and child. They fought with ropes round their necks; and when the
Confederate orders were issued that the officers of colored troops
should be put to death on capture, they took a grim satisfaction. It
helped their *esprit de corps* immensely. With us at least, there was
to be no play-soldier" (338).

In this chapter, Higginson analyzed the racial qualities of the
blacks, as he perceived them. On the whole, though he does not dis-
count their individual imperfections, Higginson's attitude to them
as a race was commendatory. Yet he was puzzled as to why "they
had not kept the land in a perpetual flame of insurrection; why, especially since the opening of the war, they had kept so still."
Higginson concluded that "the answer was to be found in the
peculiar temperament of the race, in their religious faith, and in the
habit of patience that centuries had fortified." He noted that "the
shrewder men all said substantially the same thing. What was the
use of insurrection, where everything was against them? They had
no knowledge, no money, no arms, no drill, no organization,—above all no mutual confidence." Higginson felt that,
had he been a black, his life "would have been one one long scheme of
insurrection," but he learned to respect "the patient self-control of
those who had waited till the course of events should open a better
way" (334). He was particularly fascinated by their attitude toward
their former masters, which he described as an "absence of affection" and "absence of revenge." In this moderation their religious
feelings also probably played a large part.

As to personal character, Higginson found, even among the most
ignorant, a frequent "child-like absence of vices" which he ascribed
to both innocence and inexperience. Even the experienced he found
"remarkably free from inconvenient vices," with no more or less lying or stealing "than in average white regiments" (346).
Temperance was one of their virtues. But Higginson found the
point of "greatest laxity in their moral habits" to be "the want of a
high standard of chastity." But as their sexual habits did not affect
their camp life, the colonel had little direct observation of it.
Nevertheless, he was sometimes asked to adjudicate problems

among one of his soldiers and the man's two or three "wives." In view of the dislocating effect of slavery on family life, even Higginson attached little importance to this imputed "laxity."

Higginson's greatest disappointment in the blacks involved their health. He found them easily made ill by cold, damp weather, and dust, easily fatigued and lacking resilience after injuries. This should not surprise us, since lack of protein in slave diets often led to malnutrition and low resistance to infection. Higginson remarked that "their health improved . . . as they grew more familiar with military life." But he was obliged to conclude that neither their physical nor moral temperament gave them "that toughness, that obstinate purpose of living, which sustains the less excitable Anglo-Saxon" (352 - 53). This could hardly have been an intrinsic lack in the slaves. More probably, centuries of servile dependency had made them passive rather than active, submissive rather than aggressively individualistic. In any event they satisfied their commander as equal to whites in every other respect.

The gist of the whole experience of arming these black troops for combat is contained in Higginson's remark that they "touched the pivot of the war. Whether this vast and dusky mass should prove the weakness of the nation, or its strength" depended, "in great measure, we knew, on our efforts. Till the blacks were armed, there was no guarantee of their freedom. It was their demeanour under arms that shamed the nation into recognizing them as men" (359).

VII *Afterthoughts*

Several years later, Higginson revisited Jacksonville and other scenes of his Civil War experience and appended a retrospective chapter to *Army Life.* He was pleased to recognize the social progress of the blacks, many of whom were self-employed in farming their own land, working on the steamboats, fishing, or lumbering. "What more," he asked, "could be expected of any race, after fifteen years of freedom? Are the Irish voters of New York their superiors in condition, or the factory operatives of Fall River?" (366 - 67). As he spoke to some of the veterans, Higginson came to feel that if any abuses in the treatment of the blacks existed, the remedy was "not to be found in federal interference, except in case of actual insurrection, but in the voting power of the blacks, so far as they have strength or skill to assert it and, where that fails, in their power of locomotion" (386 - 87). He believed it ungenerous, in view of the social progress made by blacks since the war, "to declare that the white people of the South have learned nothing by experience, and are 'incapable of change' " (374). Higginson believed that by 1878 the South had "reached the point where civilized methods begin to prevail" and blacks having "enlisted the laws of political economy on their side, this silent ally will be worth more than an army with banners" (387). Unfortunately, Higginson was deceived in believing that the "condition of outward peace with no conspicuous outrages" which existed in 1878 was a blessing, and he could not believe that there might be in the South "some covert plan for crushing or reenslaving the colored race" (376). Unfortunately, Jim Crow laws and other manipulations of the legal process served to institutionalize racial prejudice again and to subvert that liberty which Higginson and his black troops had fought so valiantly to achieve. Consequently, when Reconstruction failed, he was obliged to take up the cause again, though in a more pacific way—as journalist, lecturer, and legislator.

The gist of his final position on the future of blacks was rather like that of Booker T. Washington, who argued that through thrift, industry, education, and the Christian virtues blacks would eventually gain full civil, political, and constitutional rights. Self-development, the cultivation of educational opportunities, hard work, and prosperity, Washington concluded, would yield blacks a quicker entry into the mainstream of American life than radical political programs like those of W. E. B. DuBois or any of the developing black-nationalist philosophies. If Higginson's views seem conservative, hinging on the necessity of gradualism to alter the consciousness of white men, his later position was not actually retrogressive, although it seemed so to some of the current black activists. Higginson was fully committed to social and educational desegregation (achieving it for the schools in Newport), and—astonishing for a Christian minister of the time—he was even tolerant of interracial marriage. In *Part of a Man's Life*, Higginson observed that the alleged "peril" of mixed bloods "is found no longer a source of evil, this witness thinks, when concubinage has been replaced by legal marriage." He believed that "the chances are that the mingling of races will diminish, but whether this is or is not the outcome, it is, of course, better for all that this result should be legal and voluntary, rather than illegal and perhaps forced. As the memories of the slave period fade away, the mere fetich of color-phobia will cease to control our society; and marriage may come to be founded, not on the color of the skin, but upon the common courtesies of life, and upon genuine sympathies of heart and mind."[7]

Whatever may be our view of his later gradualism, *Army Life in a Black Regiment* survives the oscillation of our racial history and remains, as Howard Mumford Jones has called it, "a shrewd and sympathetic example of sociological analysis," a "forgotten masterpiece." One may disagree with Jones's assessment that "its supreme appeal is as an expression of yearning of the North for the South, for color, for warmth, for a simpler and healthier way of life than that of industrialized cities"; yet there is no doubt that "a lively humor, a fine eye for the picturesque, indignation against injustice, and real affection for his men create one of the few classics of military life in the national letters." In the case of this work, "the pen of its writer was touched with the incommunicable power that turns writing into literary art."[8]

The artistic power that informs *Army Life* was matched by a moral power in the man that generated in his troops enduring love and reverence. In a memorial tribute to him in a reunion in the 1890s, his officers remarked: "In those brave days you were not alone our commander; you were our standard also of what is noble in character. We were young and untutored; we saw in you a model of what, deep in our hearts, we aspired to be." These sentiments were shared by his enlisted men. In a letter the colonel retained until the end of his life, one of the rank-and-file privates wrote: "I meet many of the old Soldiers. I spoke of you—all hailed your name with that emotion (that become you) of the Soul when hearing of one who when in darkness burst light on their pathway."[9]

CHAPTER 4

The Liberation of Half of the Human Race: Common Sense About Women

IN his youth, Higginson once told a friend: "one thing, however, I must remember. I cannot live a past experience over again. Life is a spiral, not a circle. If I try for an instant to reproduce a past experience, except in a higher form, I shall *fail.*"[1] In this view he was reflecting the doctrine of spiritual development, of evolution upward, versified in Emerson's Motto of 1849, prefixed to *Nature:*

> A subtle chain of countless rings
> The next unto the farthest brings;
> The eye reads omens where it goes,
> And speaks all languages the rose;
> And striving to be man, the worm
> Mounts through all the spires of form.

Evolving upward through the stages of spiritual development required Higginson to pass from the achieved liberation of blacks to the question of women's cultural and legal enslavement, their rights and duties, their hopes and aspirations. Higginson's labors in behalf of woman's suffrage—a campaign deferred during the struggle to secure the freedom of blacks—had nevertheless been extremely vocal. And once the war had been concluded, Higginson and his fellow Boston reformers turned to the larger conflict—women's liberation—as a cause that involved one-half of the human race.

I *Subjects or Equals?*

Volume four of *The Writings of Thomas Wentworth Higginson* is composed of a series of essays originally published under the title *Common Sense About Women* (1881). Most of them had been periodically published in *Woman's Journal*, to which Higginson contributed and of which he was coeditor for fourteen years (1870 - 1884). Taken together, the essays in this volume constitute Higginson's major document in defense of equal rights for women.

The first essay—"Ought Women to Learn the Alphabet?" (originally published, over Lowell's resistance, in the *Atlantic*)—constitutes the ideological basis on which all of Higginson's arguments in behalf of equal rights for women were founded. Reviewing the claims, advanced throughout history, that women should be kept in a state of blissful ignorance, he raises what was for him the essential question, ought women to learn the alphabet? Should they be educated? "Concede this little fulcrum," he wrote, "and Archimedea will move the world before she has done with it: it becomes merely a question of time. Resistance must be made here or nowhere. *Obsta principiis.* Woman must be a subject or an equal: there is no middle ground."[2]

Higginson had little sympathy with the literature which claimed superiority for women, like Anthony Gibson's *A Woman's Woorth, defended against all the Men in the World, proving them to be more Perfect, Excellent, and Absolute in all Vertuous Actions than any Man of what Qualitie soever, Interlarded with Poetry* (1599). But he viewed feminists' complaints as "a perpetual protest" and the antifeminist argument a "perpetual confession." He declared that it was "too late to ignore the question; and, once opened, it can be settled only on absolute and permanent principles. There is a wrong; but where? Does woman already know too much, or too little? Was she created for man's subject, or as his equal? Shall she have the alphabet, or not?" (8)

II   *The Subjection of Women*

In Higginson's view, woman was of course created to be man's equal, and she knew too little. The obstacle to her educational, political, and social advancement he took to be "sheer contempt for the supposed intellectual inferiority of woman" (9 - 10). He had little patience with the argument that her emancipation would impair her delicacy, destroy her domesticity, or confound the distinction between the sexes. And he was dismayed that some women held that they did not need emancipation, pointing out that if individuals or classes were systematically discouraged from birth to death, they would learn, "in nine cases out of ten, to acquiesce in their degradation, if not to claim it as a crown of glory" (12).

Nor did Higginson believe that the theory of evolution argued the inevitable inferiority of women to men. Reviewing sexual differentiation in nature, Higginson observed that "the distinction of male and female is special, aimed at a certain end," but that "apart from that end, it is, throughout all the kingdoms of Nature, of minor importance" (20 - 21). Nevertheless, he believed that women's social inferiority, throughout history, had been "a legitimate thing" necessitated by primitive social conditions, a phenomenon in the "succession of civilizations." Higginson regarded the barbaric past as marked by "a reign of force" from which women necessarily could not free themselves, since they could or would not be fighters. Contrasting American women with those of other nations, Higginson asserted his belief that "Nature is endeavoring to take a new departure in the American, and to produce a race more finely organized, more sensitive, more pliable, and of more nervous energy than the races of Northern Europe" (59). In any event, the "inevitable social and moral changes" (26 - 27) which had produced civilization in nineteenth-century America had made the age ready for the equality of women. "Till the fullness of time came, woman was necessarily kept a slave to the spinning-wheel and the needle"; but now "higher work is ready; peace has brought invention to her aid, and the mechanical means for her emancipation are ready also" (26).

III   *Legal Emancipation*

In Higginson's view, the first priority was the legal emancipation of women. And that involved a redraft of legislation binding women in marriage. He dissented from Sir William Blackstone's position that "the very being and existence of the woman is suspended during marriage"; and he condemned the view, advanced by the American jurist James Kent, that "her legal existence and authority are in a manner lost" in wedlock (3). He quoted with approval William Storey's protest against the injustice of the old common law with respect to the powers and rights of married women. "The law relating to woman tends to make every family a barony or a monarchy, or a despotism, of which the husband is the baron, king, or despot, and the wife the dependent, serf, or slave," Storey argued. "That this is not always the fact is not due to the law, but to the enlarged humanity which spurns the narrow limits of its rules. The progress of civilization has changed the family from a barony to a republic; but the law has not kept pace with the advance of ideas, manners, and customs" (117). The law, in these matters, had to be changed, and changed promptly.

In particular, Higginson attacked the law which authorized the husband to appoint by his will a guardian for his children during their minority, should the husband die. This law, prevalent in many states, including Massachusetts, authorized a guardian so appointed to take the children away from their mother, at his discretion, if she remarried. Thanks to the reform agitation against this law, which could deprive children of their natural mother, the law was in due course abolished.

IV   *Woman's Suffrage*

The legal situation of women could more directly be remedied, he argued, by giving them the right to vote. Benjamin Franklin had argued that "they who have no voice nor vote in the electing of representatives do not enjoy liberty, but are absolutely enslaved to those who have votes, and to their representatives; for to be enslaved is to have governors whom other men have set over us, and be subject to laws made by the representatives of others, without having had representatives of our own to give consent in our behalf" (246). On this ground and on the principles presented in the Declaration of Independence, Higginson argued that it is "impossible to deny the natural right of women to vote, except on grounds which exclude all natural right" (250). He praised Jefferson for introducing "into a merely revolutionary document," as Lincoln put it, "an abstract truth applicable to all men and at all times"—the principle that governments derive their just power from the consent of the governed. While women generally consented to the government, Higginson argued that "the minority of women, those who wish to vote," deserve the ballot as a matter of natural right. They needed the ballot for self-protection, and he argued that the best preparation and education for suffrage was the vote itself. How she would use the ballot, when she got it, was her own affair. But Higginson believed that she would use the vote as wisely as her brothers. In any event, he was convinced that "the experience of Republican government" would be "more thoroughly tried when one-half the race is no longer disenfranchised." He was convinced that no class can trust its rights to the mercy and chivalry of any other, but that, the weaker it is, the more it needs all political aids and securities for self-protection" (285). Believing that "her traits, habits, needs, and probable demands are distinct from man," Higginson concluded that "she is not, never was, never can, and never will be, justly represented by him" (307).

V   *The Purse Strings*

Higginson took no pleasure in "the style of domestic paradise" depicted in English novels like those of Jane Austen—"half a dozen unmarried daughters running around the family hearth, all assiduously doing worsted-work and petting their papa." Therefore he argued that "a sufficiency of employment" was "the only normal and healthy condition for a human being," and it seemed proper to him that young women, if they wanted or needed work, should certainly have it. "If this additional work is done for money," he asserted, "very well. It is the conscious dignity of self-support that removes the traditional curse from labor, and a woman has a right to claim her share in that dignified position" (225).

It was the natural corollary of this argument that women should have the right to control their own fortunes, whether earned or inherited, and to develop themselves as independent beings. Higginson was far from believing marriage to be a mere business relationship, but he did regard wedlock as a "permanent co-partnership," whatever the division of labor, in which men and women should share their resources. He objected to men's controlling all of the money and obliging their wives to beg for household expenses as if it were an act of favor. "Be the joint income more or less, the wife has a claim to her honorable share, and that as a matter of right, without the daily ignominy of sending in a petition for it" (155).

Higginson was so opposed to archaic evidences of the inferior position of women that he protested against the word *obey* in the traditional marriage service. His ground was that "whoever is pledged to obey is technically and literally a slave, no matter how many roses surround the chains. All the more so if the slavery is self-imposed, and surrounded by all the prescriptions of religion. Make the marriage tie as close as church or state can make it; but let it be equal, impartial. That it may be so, the word *obey* must be abandoned or made reciprocal. Where invariable obedience is promised, equality is gone" (119 - 20). And it is worth remembering that he scandalized New England in 1855 by officiating at a marriage—that

of the radical feminist Lucy Stone—in which *obey* was conspicuous-
ly and pointedly omitted.

VI *Motherhood*

Yet Higginson did not believe that the complete woman had to
be self-supporting or employed, even in marriage. For there were
essential functions, associated with motherhood, that might prevent
her working outside the home. Motherhood was, for Higginson,
only one function, and he quoted with approval Jean Paul Richter's
observation in *Levana* that "before and after being a mother, one is
a human being; and neither the motherly nor the wifely destination
can overbalance or replace the human, but must become its means,
not its end" (37).

Even so, Higginson regarded the care of the home and the rear-
ing of children as "just as essential to building up the family fortunes as the very different toil of the outdoor partner. For young
married women to undertake any more direct aid to the family income is in most cases," he believed, "utterly undesirable, and is
asking of themselves a great deal too much" (225). In the normal
condition of things, Higginson felt that mothers already had their
hands full with home and children and should not be expected to
work outside the home as well, nor should they be charged with in-
dolence if they did not. "So sacred a thing is motherhood, so
paramount and absorbing the duty of a mother to her child, that in
a true state of society I think she should be utterly free from all
other duties,—even, if possible, from the ordinary cares of
housekeeping. If she has spare health and strength to do these other
things as pleasures, very well; but she should be relieved from them
as duties" (226 - 27).

Higginson opposed those fanatical feminists who were disrespect-
ful of the functions of motherhood. For him, "the cares of
motherhood, though not the whole duty of woman, are an essential
part of that duty, wherever they occur." In fact, in demanding suffrage for women, he claimed that they needed the vote for the sake
of their children. "To secure her in her right to them; to give her a
voice in their education; to give her a vote in the government
beneath which they are to live"—these points could not be omitted
in advancing her claims. "Anything else would be in error" (155 -
56). Higginson also warned women not to merge themselves in their
children any more than in their husbands. Whether or not free from

the chores of domesticity, wives and mothers ought to educate and develop themselves as human beings. "Even during the most absorbing years of motherhood, the wisest women still try to keep up their interest in society, in literature, in the world's affairs—were it only for their children's sake" (159). Nor did Higginson celebrate motherhood as indispensable, claiming it folly "to deny the grand and patriotic service of many women who have died and left no children among their mourners" (166).

Although Higginson worked for the full emancipation of women, he hoped that it would not result in a loss of their influence in the area of social manners. Whatever their intellectual and professional attainments, Higginson regarded women as having an important function in harmonizing social existence. "To lend joy and grace to all one's little world of friendship; to make one's house a place where every guest enters with eagerness, and leaves with reluctance; to lend encouragement to the timid, and ease to the awkward; to repress violence, restrain egotism, and make every controversy courteous,—these belong to the empire of woman." It was "a sphere so important and so beautiful" to Higginson that "even courage and self-devotion seem not quite enough, without the addition of this supremest charm" (190).

VII   *Waging the Campaign*

"As a matter of social philosophy," Higginson's train of thought led logically to "co-education, impartial suffrage, and free cooperation in all the affairs of life" (81). He urged his fellow laborers in behalf of women's liberation not to overstate their case, to be cautious in their reasoning, and to be prudent and exact in their arguments. "Woman needs equal rights, not because she is man's better half, but because she is his other half. She needs them, not as an angel, but as a fraction of humanity" (84). He quoted with approval Madame de Staël's remark, "The question is not what I want, but what I think." Henceforth, he declared, "women, like men, are to say what they think. . . . If women wish education, they must talk; if better laws, they must talk. The one chief argument against woman suffrage, with men, is that so few women even talk about it." For Higginson, "as long as the human voice can effect anything, it is the duty of women to use it; and in America, where it effects everything, they should talk all the time" (242). He urged women to master the facts of their social, legal, and educational position, to learn the arts of debate in order to present their case as well as possible, and to keep on presenting it until they were truly heard in Congress.

In England in 1878, observing Queen Victoria review the troops, Higginson noted: "I am afraid it is true that England still prefers to be ruled by a queen; and it is certain that the present sovereign will hold her prerogatives, such as they are, with a firm hand. I never find myself quite such a ruthless republican anywhere else as in England; and yet there is a certain historic satisfaction, after the long subordination of women, in thinking that the wealthiest monarchy in the world—and in some respects the foremost—takes its orders from a woman's hand."[3]

As far as the United States was concerned, Higginson was realistic enough to know that it would take time—perhaps a long time—for woman to gain the right to vote. The whole history of the "Sisterhood of Reforms" in the nineteenth century had shown that—preliminary defeats, perhaps many of them, but then victory. He had signed the call for a feminist convention first in 1850. He knew that the issue would provoke many battles. *Common Sense About Women* was published in 1881. Women received the vote in 1920, nearly forty years later, and nine years after the colonel's death. Although Higginson did not live to see his work completely done, he was confident that in due time women would be fully equals of men before the law.

CHAPTER 5

The Craft of Expression: Higginson as a Romancer, Poet, and Public Speaker

SOMETIME in 1866 or 1867, Higginson conceived a desire to make his reputation as a writer of fiction. Hawthorne, Cooper, and Irving were dead, Melville had begun to fade from public consciousness, and Howells and James had not yet begun to transform American fiction into a literature of critical Realism. Living in Newport with Mary at Mrs. Hannah Dame's boardinghouse, Higginson turned over in his mind possible subjects for a projected romance in the tradition of Hawthorne, who was, for the colonel, the greatest American writer of fiction.

I Malbone

Out of this deliberation came *Malbone: An Oldport Romance*. The genesis of the novel was Higginson's youthful disillusionment with a Divinity School friend of the 1840s, William Hurlbert. Their relationship had been a curious one. Hurlbert had impressed Higginson as a "young man so handsome in his dark beauty that he seemed like a picturesque Oriental; slender, keen-eyed, raven haired, he arrested the eye and heart like some fascinating girl." So engaging was Hurlbert that Charles Kingsley made him the hero of *Two Years Ago* and Theodore Winthrop fictionalized him in *Cecil Dreeme*. Many thought Hurlbert a "worthless fellow," but Higginson was half in love with him. The "most variously gifted and accomplished man" Higginson had ever known, who acquired "knowledge as if by magic," Hurlbert was in the end a breaker of many female hearts and "the disappointer of many high hopes,—and this in two continents." In the end Hurlbert's life was destroyed through personal licentiousness and social scandal. He fell from a "want of moral principle" into philandering, debt, and dubious practices in law.[1]

Malbone was written while several other books were "in the works"—particularly *Army Life* and a sketch of Margaret Fuller Ossoli. Yet none gave him pleasure like this romance. "To-day," he recorded in his diary, "I felt an intense longing to work on my imaginary novel. . . . The impulse was so strong that I yielded to it and got a first chapter into shape that satisfied. This was enough and afterwards I could return to the essay." As he worked on the sketch of Margaret Fuller's life, he became impatient for the opportunity to return to his story. "I know that this Romance (Malbone) is in me like the statue in the marble, for every little while I catch glimpses of parts of it here and there. I have rather held back from it, but a power within steadily forces me on; the characters are forming themselves more and more, . . . and it is so attractive to me that were it to be my ruin in fame and fortune I should still wish to keep on." His journal records his progress: "5 pages Malbone—and letter to N.Y. Standard. I have 50 pages of this novel. For the first time perhaps I have something to write which so interests me it is very hard to leave it even for necessary exercise. I hate to leave it a moment—and yet I have to write about Margaret Fuller." And later: "6 pages Ossoli. Like this very well, but grudge the time taken from Malbone, about which I was beginning to feel very happy." He remarked that he did not think that "anything except putting on uniform and going into camp has ever given me such a sense of new strange fascinating life, as the thought that I can actually construct a novel. It is as if I had learned to fly."[2] When he concluded the romance, he was baffled by what he had produced: "It is impossible for me to tell what will be thought of this book, whether it will be found too shallow or too grave, too tragic or too tame; I only know that I have enjoyed it more than anything I ever wrote (though writing under great disadvantages) and that the characters are like real men and women to me, though not one of them was, strictly speaking, imitated from life, as a whole."[3]

Malbone was partly written with the intention of populating an imagined landscape, that of Oldport, with a moving human drama. Thoreau's diary provided its epigraph: "What is Nature unless there is an eventful human life passing within her? Many joys and many sorrows are the lights and shadows in which she shows most beautiful."[4] *Malbone* undertakes to tell the story of two such eventful human lives, that of a young girl named Hope, and her betrothed lover, Philip Malbone, the titular hero of the story. Set in the old Hunter Mansion in Newport, the story narrates the return of Philip Malbone from Europe, where he has gone to retrieve Hope's sister Emilia from a reckless amour with her Swiss tutor. The story is soon told. Although engaged to Hope, Malbone has fallen in love with the impulsive Emilia, who returns his love, and he cannot resolve the dilemma in which he finds himself. To escape their predicament, Emilia marries a New York businessman, but she returns surreptitiously to Oldport and carries on an affair with Malbone in his apartment, which she reaches by way of a secret staircase in the old Victorian mansion. Hope, discovering the stairway, inadvertently surprises the two of them and immediately breaks off the engagement. Shortly thereafter, and very conveniently, Emilia is drowned while sailing with a seaman, who turns out to be the former Swiss tutor, with whom she intends to elope. Malbone meanwhile departs for Europe, an exile.

The story as such is a melodrama of betrayal in love. Malbone is presented as an attractive cad, talented, witty, and entertaining. But we are never permitted to like him, for Higginson manipulates our attitudes, turning us against him even before we have met him. He is described as having "that most perilous of all seductive natures, in which the seducer is himself seduced." He has "a personal refinement that almost amounted to purity," but he is "constantly drifting into loves more profoundly perilous than if they had belonged to a grosser man. Almost all women loved him, because he loved almost all; he never had to assume an ardor, for he always felt it." Higginson calls his heart "multi-valved": "he could love a dozen at once in various modes and gradations, press a dozen hands in a day, gaze into a dozen pairs of eyes with unfeigned tenderness; while the last pair wept for him, he was looking into the next. In truth, he loved to explore those sweet depths; humanity is the highest thing to investigate, he said, and the proper study of mankind is woman" (52). Given this "refined Mormonism of the heart," Malbone is bound to disappoint Hope's expectations. Yet because she loves him, she cannot see his moral deficiencies. And she is unwilling to believe the interpretation of his character given by Aunt Jane, who claims that Malbone has "a sort of refinement instead of principles, and a heart instead of a conscience" (45). He is, as Aunt Jane keeps saying, "too smooth, too smooth!" (46).

If Malbone is a type of the amorous villain—a Rochester or St. Elmo—Hope is hardly a character at all. Such was Higginson's devotion to the Ideal that he could not help making her an allegorical embodiment of all virtue—she is beautiful, virtuous, noble, delicate, sensitive, and long-suffering. Though deeply disappointed in love, she bears her anguish like a saint.

In an address to the reader, acknowledging that he may have disappointed us by not marrying her off, Higginson declares that not every novel must "end with an earthly marriage, and nothing be left for heaven." He observes that for girls such as Hope, "this life is given to show what happiness might be, and they await some other sphere for its fulfillment" (230). Higginson was certain that there was another sphere in which everything would "find completion, nothing omitted, nothing denied. And though a thousand oracles should pronounce this thought an idle dream, neither Hope nor I would believe them" (230 - 31). In this conclusion *Malbone* echoes dozens of domestic sentimental novels which preached self-sacrifice and submission to suffering as the lot of women. "Having been one of the Transcendentalists who revolted against Unitarian rationalism," Higginson, as Edelstein observes, "had come to conceive of the emotions as dangerous weapons requiring careful control by reason and will."[5]

Much more interesting than this conventional melodrama of love, with its cardboard characters and improbable sensational devices—the concealed stairway in the old gothic house, a love scene in the Jewish graveyard at midnight, the trance into which Emilia falls, Hope's nearly fatal accident, and the convenient disposition of the sinning woman by drowning at sea—is the portrait of social life in Newport given in *Malbone*. The manners and social rites of the wealthy, their carriage rides, and their balls and dances gave Higginson a rich opportunity to satirize snobbishness and parvenu social pretension. Among the vulgarians, the "gentlemen" cannot be told from the waiters, and the "ladies" are guilty of bad manners. Stray widows, visiting royalty, and rootless matrons "with a tendency to corpulence and good works" (76), like Mrs. Brash, compose the visiting list, while the men are generally in town on business. For Aunt Jane, Newport life in the summer is amusing "though the society is nothing but a pack of visiting-cards. In winter it is too dull for young people, and only suits quiet old women like me, who merely live here to keep the Ten Commandments and darn their stockings" (16).

Higginson also satirized the education of young women in polite society. Taught at boarding schools by governesses and coming out at eighteen, what could they know? Implicitly at least, the novel calls for a more rigorous education fitting young women for the life of the intellect as well as for that of the family and society.

The materialism of the plutocracy and the mindless indifference to literature and ideas among the very rich are also attacked in this novel. Malbone speaks for his author in asking, "Who cares for literature in America . . . after a man rises three inches above the newspaper level? Nobody reads Thoreau; only an insignificant fraction can read Emerson or even Hawthorne. The majority of people have hardly even heard their names" (94). "What inducement has a writer?" asks Malbone, as if he were Higginson.

Yet not even Higginson's ridicule of plutocratic vulgarity and American antiintellectualism saves *Malbone* from hopeless mediocrity. While writing the romance, he felt himself powerfully moved by his imagination, but Higginson could not even tell a story as well as popular contemporaries like Maria Cummins or Mrs. E. D. E. N. Southworth. In his introduction Higginson had remarked that "one learns, in growing older, that no fiction can be so strange nor appear so improbable as would the simple truth," and that "no man of middle age can dare trust himself to portray life in its full intensity, as he has studied or shared it; he must resolutely set aside as indescribable the things most worth describing, and must expect to be charged with exaggeration, even when he tells the rest" (4). He claimed realism for his tale by pointing out that the secret stairway in the old Victorian mansion really existed, that Aunt Jane (modeled on his wife Mary) and Malbone were "studied as closely as possible from real life" (iv). Yet the effect of his work is far from realism. Higginson was committed to ideality in literature, and Hawthorne was his model. Hope, for example, is a Georgiana-figure, a "noble girl, who walks the earth fresh and strong as a Greek goddess, pure as Diana, stately as Juno" (36). Higginson observed that "all sacredness and sweetness, all that was pure and brave and truthful, seem to rest in her" (70).

The genteel public could not have objected to his characterization or to his moral, but they did not warm to his art. He noted that the book was received by the public "with quiet approbation . . . though not with eagerness."[6] The critics were less approbative. The *Nation* called it thin and the *Examiner and London Review* remarked, "If this book had been published anonymously, we should have said that it was written by an American lady who had carefully studied George Sand and Nathaniel Hawthorne."[7]

Partly in self-justification, Higginson later wrote that *Malbone* "was written in some degree as a relief during a prolonged period of peculiar care and anxiety." Yet though his care for his invalid wife Mary must have been a burdensome ordeal, his escape into imagination was not felicitous. He himself recognized this, in due course, and remarked that the faults of *Malbone* "are obvious enough, and the recognition of them has kept the author from again risking himself so far in the realms of fiction" (iv).

One of the obvious faults of *Malbone* is the heavy didacticism of its conclusion. The moral is so explicit that we could not conceivably mistake Higginson's purposes. And its complexity and ambiguity are considerably lessened by Higginson's not granting us the privilege of drawing our own inferences. In due course he came to see the uselessness of such tacked-on moralizing. In "Discontinuance of the Guide-Board," published many years later in *Book and Heart: Essays on Literature and Life* (1899), Higginson revealed that he had learned something from the Realists—like Howells and James—about the relation of morality to fiction. Noting that "fiction is drawing nearer to life," Higginson concluded that "in real life, as we see it, the moral is usually implied and inferential, not painted on a board; you must often look twice, or look many times, in order to read it." He took satisfaction in Hamlin Garland's "A Branch-Road" in *Main-Travelled Roads* for its deliberate avoidance of an explicit moral, even though the tale dealt with adultery, observing that "the writer of fiction should surely be allowed henceforth to wind up his story in his own way, without formal proclamation of his moral; or, better still, to leave the tale without technical and elaborate winding up, as nature leaves her stories."

Higginson was of course aware that the inattentive reader might very well miss the significance of the tale if the writer did not spell it out. And he was aware that good novels might be classed as immoral "simply because the guide-board is omitted and the reader left to draw his own moral." Yet more and more, Higginson felt the propriety of relying on "the presumption of brains" in the reader. Realism, he wrote, "has since achieved its maturity, and undoubtedly has won—if it has not already lost again—possession of the field." The rise of Realism, he thought, was merely a swing in the pendulum, rather than a permanent change, but he held that if we excuse Realism, "as we plainly must, from the perpetuation of the guide-board, we can only ask that it shall go on and do its work so well that no such aid shall be needed; that its moral, where there is one, shall be reasonably plain; that is, so clearly put as to produce a minimum of misunderstanding."

Even so, Higginson thought that realistic fiction should "stop short of undesirable materials." In any event, readers some "fifty or sixty years ago in America" obtained, he thought, "some of their very best tonic influences through . . . thoroughly ideal tales" with an explicit moral. Even though such stories were didactic, "their moral was irresistible for those who really cared enough for the books to read them; they needed no guide-boards; the guide-board was for the earlier efforts at realism, before it had proved its strength."[8]

Yet despite its overt didacticism, *Malbone* always had a special place in Higginson's literary affections—though he never again tried a longer work of fiction. Many years later, after he had moved back to Cambridge, on the occasion of the publication of the English edition of the novel, Higginson revisited the setting of *Malbone:* "Walked along the bay, beside the empty houses, and the dismantled house where I wrote Malbone. The fog bell tolled and the whole scene was full of ghosts; how long it seemed since those dreamy summers! That was the ideal epoch of my life: I have written nothing like that since and may not again."[9] On looking back at his career as a romancer, Higginson remarked in 1900 that "it is rather a relief to his conscience that he has never shared, on any larger scale, either the disheartening discouragements or the more perilous successes of the novelist" (iv).

II   Oldport Days

Oldport Days is a series of seven sketches which record the local color of the Newport area where Higginson lived from 1864 - 1878. It communicates the atmosphere of Newport in the off-season, after the summer tourists have departed. He took a Republican's delight in the social rivalries of the summer parvenus, as the "aristocrats" of Boston, Philadelphia, and New York vied for social position in the town during the summer. "The boast of heraldry, the pomp of power, are doubtless good things to have in one's house," he remarks, "but are cumbrous to travel with. Meeting here on central ground, partial aristocracies tend to neutralize each other. A Boston family comes, bristling with generalities, and making the most of its little all of two centuries. Another arrives from Philadelphia, equally fortified in local heraldries unknown in Boston. A third from New York brings a briefer pedigree, but more gilded. Their claims," he concluded, "are incompatible," for "there is no common standard, and so neither can have precedence. Since no human memory can retain the great-grandmothers of three cities, we are practically as well off as if we had no great-grandmothers at all."[10] Higginson relished the "new" in Oldport, "the liveries, the incomes, the manners" (268), for he found "a delicious freshness about these exhibitions." But *Oldport Days* records the satisfaction of the permanent residents once the season had ended, the great hotels had been closed, and the four-in-hand, with its liveried servants and trunks, had departed for the station.

The colonel had a minor poet's eye for the picturesque and eccentric social types left remaining after the departure of the summer visitors—the fishermen, the woodsmen, the retired sea captains, and the "reduced gentlewomen" of the town, "quiet maiden ladies of seventy, with perhaps a tradition of beauty and bellehood" (280), practicing their small economies as they purchased provisions in the local grocery. Like the fishermen and "tradespeople living under summer gains" (272), Higginson found the off-season more pleasing than the summer, and he celebrated the "spirit of repose" pervading the nearly deserted streets of Oldport. These sketches give a sense of the picturesque, the dreamy, the remote and isolated that characterize the best of local-color writing.

A hymn of celebration to the pastimes of autumn and winter life in Newport—the fishing on the long wharves, the clam digging, the cutting and storing of firewood, winter tramps across the great estates of the wealthy—*Oldport Days* presents a particular sensibility taking pleasure in the little-noticed and seemingly insignificant aspects of the common life in New England. "Oldport Wharves" is a typical sketch, some twenty pages of text being devoted to a description of the wharves and pilings, the texture of the water as it ebbed and flowed, the history of the harbor, the etymology of its name, and its centrality as the launching point of the town's major off-season industry. Higginson's personality, his poetic sensibility, and his charm carry the whole piece, which is important for the tone, the mood, and the atmosphere created by the texture of the language. In "A Driftwood Fire," a comparable piece, paragraph after paragraph is devoted to Higginson's meditation on fires and fireplaces, on varieties of driftwood, techniques for collecting it, and the reveries induced by gazing into the flames.

"In a Wherry" is a tone poem to the spiritual satisfactions of row-
ing in the bay and drifting in the harbor while Higginson con-
templates the surrounding nature. He is most clearly the
Transcendental naturalist, like Thoreau, in his minute examination
of the land and seascape. Many of the observations in *Oldport Days*
suggest his indebtedness to the gnomic style of Emerson, the Concord master. He observes that "most men do their work out of doors
and their dreaming at home; and those whose work is done at home
need something like a wherry in which to dream out of doors"
(360). In this sketch, Higginson drifts with us from place to place
along the shores of Newport, observing the movement of the winds
and water, the fowl and fish life. Witnessing a kingfisher diving for
his catch, he remarks: "The best observer in the end is not he who
works at the microscope or telescope most unceasingly, but he
whose nature becomes sensitive and receptive, drinking in
everything . . ." (360).

Oldport Days is a record of such meditations on nature, as
witnessed by a sensitive and receptive observer who drank in
everything. For Higginson, the light and the tides were the "silvery
whispers in which Nature ever spoke to man" (363). Every aspect of
the natural scene suggested to him spiritual correspondences
touching the quality and meaning of life. In their way these
sketches, like Monet paintings, impressionistically pictorialize "the
wonderful shifting of expression that touches even a thing so essentially unchanging as the sea" (374).

How the aspect of nature induced in him reflections on reality is
suggested by "A Moonglade." Here his point of departure is "that
path of light which lies beneath the moon upon the sea, and which
appears to slope down from the horizon to the place where each
observer stands" (392). This nocturnal phenomenon at sea
suggested to him the beauty and uniqueness of the individual's
angle of vision. "Were this shore lined with ten thousand observers,
each would see a separate moonglade. The ocean is in reality
covered with one vast sheet of light; but each man looks upon it at
one angle, and possesses for himself that particular line of luster
traced from the horizon to his eyes. When a boat drifts across that
track, he fancies that it has only just now become visible, because
he now sees it; yet at each moment the boat was visible to
somebody, in the rays of the self-same moon." Higginson felt it to
be thus in our lives: "each has a separate glimpse of the life of every
other; the look you see in some person's face at this moment, caught

for an instant only, is there for you alone; it will never precisely occur again, as it never occurred before; and if you had skill to depict
it, you might make it immortal. So many millions of people, so
many millions of moments in the life of each; and yet that one moment of the million, caught and fixed forever by Shakespeare or
Browning, secures its permanent record, like a instantaneous
photograph of the sea. The strange and haunting expression on the
face of Mona Lisa, in the Louvre,—first disappointing, then allur-
ing, always eluding,—was doubtless the fruit of a single brief
glimpse at some face as variable and as inexhaustible in its changes
as is yonder moonglade on the bay" (397 - 98).

III   Nature Essays

Higginson's nature studies in *Oldport Days* constitute only a fraction of his essay studies in the flora and fauna of Cambridge and
Newport. Brought up in the milieu that shaped Thoreau, and
warmly appreciative of Thoreau's *A Week on the Concord and
Merrimack Rivers, Walden,* and *The Maine Woods,* Higginson
achieved a considerable reputation in his own right as a familiar essayist of Nature and her ways. Most of his nature studies, published
first in the *Atlantic* and collected in *Outdoor Papers* and *The
Procession of the Flowers,* exceeded Thoreau's in popularity.
Among the most memorable are "April Days," "Water-Lilies,"
"My Out-door Study," "Snow," and "The Life of Birds."

These familiar essays, like those in *Oldport Days,* are elegant, im-
pressionistic studies of the commoner glories of the woods and
shore. Steeped in the love of Nature, they reveal an attentive
witness of minute events in the seasonal cycle, and a deeply
thoughtful man meditating the "lessons of faith and beauty" to be _
derived from the immersion of the self in Nature. His attitudes
toward the rivers and streams, the woods and fields, are those of the
modern conservationist and ecologist. But pervading these essays is
a deeper reverence for Nature, based on its manifestation of the
noumenal Divine Spirit, that revelation through the phenomenal of
what Emerson in *Nature* had called the "Universal Spirit." "These
essays on Nature," he told Harriet Prescott, "delight me so infinite-
ly that all other themes seem tiresome beside them; I am sure that I
have never come so near to Nature . . . and therefore never so truly
and deeply lived; and sometimes I feel so Exalted in this nearness
that it seems as if I never could sorrow any more." He wrote from

"pure enjoyment," he told her, "spending days and weeks on single sentences."[11]

IV *Higginson's Poetic Effusions*

I have already remarked, in chapter one, that young Higginson underwent considerable *sturm und drang* over whether he should devote his life to poetry. In due course, his limitations became obvious to him, and he turned to more pressing considerations like reform and literary criticism. Nevertheless, during the course of his long career, Higginson published a number of poems which established him as no worse and considerably better than the flood of contemporary versifiers "immortalized" in E. C. Stedman's *An American Anthology, 1787 - 1900*, the turn-of-the-century touchstone of American poetic greatness. Among Higginson's volumes of published poems are *Thalatta* (1853), *The Afternoon Landscape: Poems and Translations* (1889), and—the modesty of the title is becoming—*Such as They Are: Poems* (1893). Gathered in 1900 in volume six of the collected writings, they were dedicated to his schoolmate James Russell Lowell.

Such as they are, these verses reveal Higginson to be steeped in the Romantic tradition, sentimental, formalist in meter, rhyme, and stanzaic structure, and preoccupied with themes of exalted spirituality—in short, a minor poet of the Genteel Tradition. Among those perhaps worth reading are "Ode to a Butterfly," "Sonnet to Duty," "Since Cleopatra Died," and "Sixty and Six." Of these, the writer's favorite is the last, which is devoted to his daughter Margaret Waldo, who had been born to the childless man in his old age. Not a good poem, yet the sheer joy in his daughter lifts it above banality—at least for the reader sympathetic to an elderly father of a young girl.

More expressive of Higginson's intellectual views are poems like the "Sonnet to Duty," "To John Greenleaf Whittier," and "Waiting for the Bugle." Memorable too are certain occasional lines—like the apostrophe in his poem to Helen Hunt Jackson, "O soul of fire within a woman's clay!"; or this from his poem to Edward Bellamy, "Heirs of Time": "I hear the tread of marching men, / The patient armies of the poor"; or this meditation on the expression of the Sistine Madonna: "What says it? All that life / Demands of those who live, to be and do,— / Calmness, in all its bitterest, deepest strife; / Courage, till all is through." Probably

the best sustained passage Higginson ever composed, however, was
the concluding sestet of "Since Cleopatra Died":

> . . . Ah, Love and Pain
> Make their own measure of all things that be.
> No clock's slow ticking marks their deathless strain;
> The life they own is not the life we see;
> Love's single moment is eternity:
> Eternity, a thought in Shakespeare's brain.

For all the grace of an occasional felicitous line, Higginson's
verses are didactic, sentimental, archaic in diction, and flawed by
inversions in syntax that were already obsolete by mid-century.
Still, Higginson regarded himself as a serious man of letters whose
criticism of verse in his time could not have been so well informed
had he not himself tried to kindle the divine flame of poetry.

V   Translations

Two of the pieces in *Oldport Days*—"Sunshine and Petrarch"
and "An Artist's Creation"—diverge from the basic plan of the
book. The former is a meditation of the "consummate beauty of
. . . earthly things" (377) in the light of Petrarch's poetic vision of
Laura. Meditating upon the landscape in Oldport provided Higginson with a pretext for presenting translations of about a dozen
Petrarchan sonnets and *canzone*. His translations are ultimately
limited by their cloying Victorian lushness and melodic lyricism. He
may have understood his limitations as a translator, but he
acknowledges the translator's difficulty only in general terms—as
anyone's intrinsic problem in trying to transpose into another
language the complex art of poetic expression. He notes that
"Goethe compared translators to carriers, who convey good wine to
market, though it gets unaccountably watered by the way." He felt
it "absurd" to try to translate truly great poetry, and he raised the
question as to why, if we appreciate a great poem, we should not
leave it alone, in its original language. "It is a doubtful blessing to
the human race, that the instinct of translation still prevails,
stronger than reason; and after one has once yielded to it, then each
untranslated favorite is like the trees round the backwoodsman's
clearing, each of which stands, a silent defiance, until he has cut it
down" (380). This image conveys a peculiarly violent conception of
the translator's difficult task, but so Higginson saw the problem and

so he laid his ax to the root of Petrarch's tree. The translated effect of this theory, while interesting, is not altogether felicitous. The best is the translation of Sonnet 309 ("*Dicemi spesso il mio fidato speglio*"):

> Oft by my faithful mirror I am told,
> And by my mind outworn and altered brow,
> My earthly powers impaired and weakened now,—
> "Deceive thyself no more, for thou art old!"
> Who strives with Nature's laws is over-bold,
> And Time to his commandment bids us bow.
> Like fire that waves have quenched, I calmly vow
> In life's long dream no more my sense to fold.
> And while I think, our swift existence flies,
> And none can live again earth's brief career,—
> Then in my deepest heart the voice replies
> Of one who now has left this mortal sphere,
> But walked alone through earthly destinies,
> And of all women is to fame most dear.

Though quaintly Elizabethan in its tone, the translation sufficiently conveys the immortality that "genius may confer upon the objects of its love" (390).

VI   *Short Stories*

"An Artist's Creation" in *Studies in Romance* is a Hawthornean parable about a painter's obsession with his art, his wife's utter devotion to his genius, and the peculiar situation of their young daughter, who is excluded from the magic circle of her parents' love for each other. Laura, the wife and mother in this sketch, is devoted to her husband with an intensity that, ambiguously, is either "ideal" or else the expression of "a kind of duplex selfishness, so profound and so undisguised as to make one shudder."[12] Her husband, Kenmure, is completely preoccupied with his art and his wife. Both ignore the child, Marian, who plays about their feet. In the end, Laura dies and Kenmure and little Marian are left alone. In a fit of depression, Kenmure asserts the futility of his art, since —despite his sketches and paintings of Laura—he has achieved "no real memorial of her presence, nothing to perpetuate the most beautiful of lives" (355). In a denouement that rivals Dickens in sentimentality, the little girl Marian at that moment creeps into

Kenmure's arms, and it becomes apparent to him (it has been apparent to the reader all along) that the daughter is the true perpetuation of Laura, that it is *she* who is the "artist's creation."

No better or worse than hundreds of comparable nineteenth-century didactic tales, "An Artist's Creation" is yet a failure, since it trades so shamelessly on the sentimental figure of the neglected child. Only a childless man could have written this story; and only a writer with a deep conflict over the rival claims of morality and aesthetics could have so emphasized the dangers to the moral sensibility of a life devoted to art. Higginson's attitude toward art, however, was a tolerably meditated one. Emerson had once observed, "Better that the books should be not quite so good, and the bookmaker abler and better and not himself often a ludicrous contrast to all that he has written." About this observation Higginson remarked: "Perhaps no sentence . . . ever influenced my life so much as this about 1844. It has made me willing to vary my life and work for personal development, rather than to concentrate it and sacrifice myself to a specific result."[13] Perfection of the life or the work—thus Yeats put the artist's dilemma. As men and women, we may admire Higginson's life, but there can be no doubt that his effort to perfect it, through devoting himself to varied causes, diminished the focus and intensity of his fiction and verse.

Malbone and *Oldport Days* were reprinted together, in 1900, as volume five of the collected edition, under the title *Studies in Romance*. Published with them was a short story entitled "The Monarch of Dreams" (1886). Since these three works were "the product of what was perhaps the most imaginative period of his life," Higginson felt that they "naturally belonged together. . . ."[14] "The Monarch of Dreams" is the story of Francis Ayrault, who has secluded himself in the remote back country of New England in order to recuperate from "a series of domestic cares and watchings" which had "almost broken him down." In a remark that makes Ayrault seem very much like his creator, whose deceased wife Mary had been a complete invalid, Higginson observed that "nothing debilitates a man of strong nature like the too prolonged and exclusive exercise of the habit of sympathy" (236).

Ayrault is therefore a man who needs complete rest and change. He is alone in life except for "a little sunbeam of a sister, the child of his father's second marriage." As befits the Hawthornean allegory, the little five-year-old girl is named Hart. In his isolation from human society, Frank Ayrault becomes "absorbed in a project too fantastic to be talked about, yet which had really done more than anything else to bring him to that lonely house" (238). Here, virtually detached from all human ties, he has resolved "to make a mighty effort at self-concentration, and to render himself what no human being had ever yet been,—the ruler of his own dreams" (239). Obsessed by the nature of dreams, Ayrault studies the way his own dreams connect themselves and how the mind can banish a nightmare by compelling itself to remember that the nightmare is unreal. Ayrault varies his sleeping conditions so as to create different sequences of dream thought. He comes to feel that "dreams could be made to recur by . . . conscious thought" (243). Having studied a photograph of Mont-Saint-Michel, Ayrault one night experiences a dream of lying full-length on a steep, grassy slope like that in Normandy. The next night he has a similar dream, but on this occasion the slope is "covered with human beings,—men, women, and children—all trying to pursue various semblances of occupation; but all clinging to the short grass" (246). The similarities between these two dreams induce him to believe that he has, "by an effort of the will, formed a connection between two dreams" (247).

Agitated by this phenomenon, he abandons his little sister Hart to the nurse and becomes obsessed in his experiment with dreams. On successive nights he sees himself on a vast plain surrounded by people. Not unexpectedly, there was "a singular want of all human relation in the tie between himself and all these people" in the dream. "He felt as if he had called them into being, which indeed he had; and could annihilate them at pleasure, which perhaps could not be so easily done." He discovers "a certain hardness in his state of mind toward them; indeed, why should a dreamer feel patience or charity or mercy toward those who exist but in his mind? Ayrault at any rate felt none; the sole thing which disturbed him was that they sometimes grew a little dim, as if they might vanish and leave him unaccompanied. When this happened, he threw with conscious volition a gleam of light over them and thereby refreshed their life. They enhanced his weight in the universe: he would no more have parted with them than a Highland chief with his clansmen" (251 - 52).

Night after night, Ayrault dominates his dreams—fancying himself in "legislative halls where men were assembled by hundreds, waiting for him"; in "libraries, where the books belonged to him, and whole alcoves were filled with his own publications"; and in "galleries of art, where he had painted many of the pictures and selected the rest." In these dreams he is truly a monarch, for there are no equals, only menials and subordinates, about him. Gradually, all of the people begin to resemble one another and eventually it comes to him that they resemble himself. Suddenly his dreams are populated by "innumerable and uncontrollable beings, everyone of whom was Francis Ayrault." These figures divide and multiply, populating and repopulating his dreamworld. "Worst of all, each one of these had as much apparent claim to his personality as he himself possessed. He could no more retain his individual hold upon his consciousness than the infusorial animalcule in a drop of water can know to which of its subdivided parts the original individuality attaches" (254).

Meanwhile, little Hart falls ill and grows pale and thin, neglected by her brother. Though traces of human sympathy flicker in him, Ayrault continues to be obsessed by the people in his dreams, who gradually grow smaller and smaller until they are eventually "no larger than the heads of pins" (256). As the days go on, the nursemaid Susan repeatedly warns Ayrault about the child Hart, and finally proposes taking her into her own room. "She does not get sound sleep, sir; she complains of her dreams." "Of what dreams?" said Ayrault. "Oh, about you, sir," was the reply; "she sees you very often, and a great many people who look just like you" (256). Ayrault is horrified to think that not only is his own dream life haunted by these creatures of his own invention but that the child herself has been invaded by his dreams. Like Hawthorne's Aylmer, Ayrault is tempted, "for a moment, to employ this un-spoiled nature in the perilous path of experiments on which he had entered" (256 - 57). He resists the temptation, however, but cannot escape his entanglement "in the meshes of a dreamlife that had become a nightmare."

The townspeople solicit Ayrault's assistance in solving various local problems, and although he is momentarily sympathetic, he always manages to avoid giving the needed help. The most stirring appeal to his sympathy occurs at the outbreak of the Civil War. When the call comes for troop enlistments, Ayrault promises to enlist and encourages thereby several other men in the neighborhood to do the same. In the decisive act, Ayrault feels himself free of the nightmare visions: "He felt himself a changed being. . . . What had he to do now with that pale dreamer who had nourished his absurd imaginings until he had barely escaped being controlled by them . . . . No matter: he was now free, and the spell was broken. Life, action, duty, honor, a redeemed nation, lay before him; all entanglements were cut away" (260). That night, on the news of a great defeat which requires immediate reinforcements, those who had pledged themselves to enlist are summoned to the train depot. While Ayrault's comrades assemble for departure, he is at home in his chamber, "beset, encircled, overwhelmed," by "the mob of unreal beings" which have invaded anew his dream-life. As he dreams, confused sounds come from without of "the rolling of railway wheels, the scream of locomotive engines, the beating of drums, the cheers of men, the report and glare of fireworks." Vaguely aware of the repeated sound of knocking at his door, Ayrault lies embroiled in the tumult of the figures in his dream, who "increase steadily in size, even as they had before diminished; and the waxing was more fearful than the waning. From being Gulliver among the Lilliputians, Ayrault was Gulliver in Brobdingnag. Each image of himself, before diminutive, became colossal: they blocked his path; he actually could not find himself, could not tell which was he that should arouse himself, in their vast and endless self-multiplication" (262 - 63). Gradually the shouts subside as the train moves away. And Ayrault is left alone, in isolation and in darkness.

It takes very little subtlety, and no knowledge of Freud's *On the Interpretation of Dreams*, to perceive that this story, like Hawthorne's "Ethan Brand," deals with the dangers to the moral life of withdrawal from the human community, or what Hawthorne called the "magnetic chain of humanity." Ayrault's is the sin of the obsessive idea, what Hawthorne called "the sin of an intellect that triumphed over the sense of brotherhood with man and reverence for God, and sacrificed everything to its own mighty claims!" In his neglect of Hart, or human sympathy, in his indifference to the needs of the community, and in his failure to commit himself to a life of action in defense of his country, he commits, for Higginson, the unpardonable sin.

Yet below the manifest content of the story lies a latent significance still more troubling. In its way the story betrays a radical doubt as to Higginson's real identity. Preacher, poet, soldier, suffragist, temperance crusader—which was the real Higginson? Moreover, the story is a veiled self-indictment of the temptation, which Higginson must often have felt, to cast off the burden of constant attention to and sympathy for his invalid wife Mary and to all humanitarian causes, and to immerse himself in the life of the imagination. Ayrault's dreams, like those imaginative reveries which produced *Malbone,* constituted a fantasy escape from a perhaps temporarily unendurable domestic reality.

At the deepest level of his being, however, Higginson was unable to accept the possibility that the artist might be an isolato whose ultimate purpose in life is to traffic with the creations of his own imagination. Like Hawthorne, Higginson feared that the life of the artist—withdrawn, solitary, introverted by its preoccupation with invention—might be the real unforgivable sin. Consequently, he resisted the inducements of his own imagination and willfully devoted himself to social service and reform. Like "An Artist's Creation," therefore, "The Monarch of Dreams" conveys a deep distrust of the life devoted to art; these stories urge, albeit indirectly, the necessity of the individual's total involvement in the community about him. Better a perfection of the life than the work. In any event Higginson called the story his "favorite child"—largely because it was the only piece of his the *Atlantic* ever rejected. His family thought it "weird" and "morbid," and he apologized for printing it. But he felt it to be "the first strong bit of purely imaginative work I ever did," and he observed, "I like to do things in order to know that I can do them; and the old spirit of adventurousness still lives in me." He took eventual satisfaction that "it has been more praised by many than anything I ever did—including very cool critics like [James Russell] Lowell and [Charles Eliot] Norton."[15]

VII   *On the Platform*

Among Higginson's other talents was an extraordinary gift for public speaking. So successful was he among his contemporaries that he even wrote a brief manual about the platform art, *Hints on Writing and Speech-making.* Noting that the secret of great oratory is to be passionately committed to your subject, he argued that "even the actor on the dramatic stage must fill himself with his part, or he is nothing, and the public speaker on the platform must be more than a dramatic actor to produce the highest effects." Belief in the cause proclaimed gave a "profound sincerity" to the delivery which helped to overcome "the obstacles of a hoarse voice, a stammering tongue, or a feeble presence."[16] When Harvard students asked him how to master political oratory, he invariably told them to "Enlist in a reform." As Howard Mumford Jones has remarked, "Anger at the fugitive slave law condensed Higginson's prose into forcefulness." But it did not end there. His "narrative energy" throughout all of his works was "in turn a function of moral zeal."[17]

Higginson observed of the antislavery platform that no one who spoke on behalf of abolition was a really poor speaker, that (in Emerson's words) "eloquence was dog-cheap" in Boston. The reason was simple: "the cause was too real, too vital, too immediately pressing upon the heart and conscience, for the speaking to be otherwise than alive. . . . How could eloquence not be present there, when we had not time to think of eloquence?"[18] His platform teachers, his instructors in oratory, were those slaves whom he first saw "walking clumsily across the platform, just arrived from the South, . . . whom I saw develop in the course of years into the dignity of freedom. What were the tricks of oratory in the face of men and women like these? We learned to speak because their presence made silence impossible."[19]

On the abolition platform and in lyceum lectures in the antebellum period, Higginson taught himself to organize and deliver coherent lectures without notes, since he felt that "a speaker's magnetic hold upon his audience is unquestionably impaired by the slightest bit of paper in his hand." Although the profession of lecturing was "benumbing to the mind as well as exhausting to the body,"[20] Higginson nevertheless found it an "antidote for provincialism." Lecturing throughout the East and West, Higginson was exposed to almost every level of American culture, every social class, every profession and activity in the country. This wide exposure confirmed him in his passionate republicanism. Although the lecture system was eventually to fade away with the spread of newspapers and the theater, Higginson continued his oratory in the Massachusetts Legislature in the 1880s, where he was credited with the success of many acts of legislation.

In sum, Higginson was a master of public speaking and a teacher of the forensic art. He felt that the nemesis of public speaking—"the thing which makes it seem almost worthless in the long run—is the impossibility of making it tell for anything after its moment is passed." While he who produces a book has produced something that will last, "the popular orator soon disappears from memory." Higginson felt that the brief fame of the platform orator was compensated for by the dramatic excitement of his life. Although the writer's work lasted longer, Higginson felt that "at favored moments," the orator can rise "to some height of enthusiasm that shall make all his previous structure of preparation superfluous; as the ship in launching glides from the waves, and scatters cradled timbers and wedges on the waters that are henceforth to be her home."[21]

CHAPTER 6

The Craft of Herodotus:
Higginson as an Historian

EMERSON had said in "History" that "broader and deeper we must write our annals,—from an ethical reformation, from an influx of the ever new, ever sanative conscience,—if we would trulier express our central and wide-related nature, instead of this old chronology of selfishness and pride to which we have too long lent our eyes." Emerson expressed dissatisfaction with the aridity of historical prose, with the "dissector" and the "antiquary." Properly interpreted, he concluded, "history no longer shall be a dull book."[1] For Emerson, and many of his contemporaries, history was the lengthened shadow of the great man; it was, therefore, inseparable from biography. Without ever formulating a clear position on historiography, Higginson shared in the feeling that history and biography so overlapped; and in Higginson's own writing the modern critic will find it difficult to know whether he should classify some of the prose as works of history or biography.

Nevertheless, the colonel was much interested in the American past and in the personae who had stood at the center of great national events. He shared Emerson's feeling that history must be written more broadly and deeply, less dully and more interestingly, from the ethical perspective of the "ever sanative conscience." As a youth at Harvard he had studied the great historians—Thucydides, Caesar, Herodotus, Gibbon, and others. And he knew Bancroft, Prescott, Parkman, and Motley. History appealed to him, and in the early years of his career he wrote a number of slight historical sketches for the *Atlantic Monthly*. Forced to live on the income from such articles, he had no time to deal comprehensively with our annals.

I *Juvenile History*

But in the early 1870s, Higginson was approached by a Boston educator, George B. Emerson, to write "an attractive juvenile history of the United States." Emerson gave Higginson an advance of one thousand dollars to cover his family expenses while he completed the book. Writing this juvenile history was a totally novel experience, for he had never done a comprehensive, fully researched history and had never composed for such an audience. For more than a year, Higginson accumulated material and attempted to reduce it into compact, intelligible form. His diary records that on one day of research he wrote ten postcards in "10 languages—English, French, Spanish, Italian, Portuguese, German, Swedish, Latin, Greek, and Hebrew." He told one of his correspondents that he did not know whether the work would "be readable after all." In fact, the first draft was not—the style was *too* juvenile. And he was obliged to spend a second year revising it.

On completing the *Young Folks' History of the United States* (1875), he told a friend that it was "a relief to me at last to have this work done, as it pressed on me a good deal, and especially this month. On the whole I have rather enjoyed it, though so long continued a work. . . . I should not have a doubt [as to its success] were it written by any one else. My luck may turn but I don't think I was born to be rich. I have had to economize unusually these last two years, for Mr. Emerson's $1000 has been far from compensation for the time I have given. And unless I clear something beyond that first $1000 which goes to him, I shall be out of pocket." Nevertheless, he concluded, "it will be pleasant to think, in any case, that I have done something to make American history clear and attractive."[2]

Unexpectedly, the *Young Folks' History* was credited with inaugurating "a new era in writing history for children," and it became greatly popular. Its appeal puzzled Higginson, for although the work "so often (certainly) dragged in the writing," yet it was found "universally attractive in the reading." His publishers, Lee and Shepard, told him that they expected to sell forty thousand copies the first year and two hundred thousand in all. And when Emerson canceled the thousand-dollar advance, and the publishers proposed that he write "a manual of Universal History," Higginson recorded in his diary: "I think I have now for the first time accepted the fact that I have achieved a worldly success at last and may really have those additional few hundred dollars a year that would seem wealth to me. Perhaps even this year I may. . . . It does not excite me, but I confess to agreeable sensations." Unfortunately, Lee and Shepard failed three months later and the "convenient little cup" of wealth slipped from his hands. Nevertheless, eventually translated into French, German, and Italian, and put into braille, the *Young Folks' History* became Higginson's most popular historical work. Adopted by school systems across the country, it became a standard school textbook on American history. Its popularity was summed up by one eight-year-old boy, the son of a Harvard professor, who told Higginson, "I like your History of the United States about as well as the Odyssey."[3]

If today the work does not stand up to Homer, it does surpass the drier histories of Timothy Pitkin and Abiel Holmes then generally available to young people. Its distinction is that it was the first juvenile history to cover comprehensively the discovery and settlement of the country from the era of the Norsemen to the present. (Successive revisions—in 1882, 1886, 1896, and 1910—brought it up to Cleveland's second term.) The special achievement of the work was that it aimed "to tell the story of the United States in a clear and simple manner for young and old." In writing the book Higginson adopted two rules: "to omit all names and dates not really needful and to make liberal use of the familiar traits and incidents of everyday."[4] Relying on the element of human interest, heightened through anecdote and illustration, quotation and dramatic scene, Higginson produced what J. S. Bassett has called "patriotic history"—that type of historical writing which aims to induce in the reader admiration for his country and its leaders, to gratify his appetite for information about his country, and to please by its noble, elevated style.[5]

The writing of this work eventually led Higginson to theorize about his task in two significant essays—"Why Do Children Dislike History?" and "History in Easy Lessons." Lecturing the profession on the utility of humanizing the facts so that pleasure, as well as instruction, could result, he observed that history, properly told, is "but a series of tales of human beings." In *Young Folks' History of the United States*, he vivified his story by avoiding the dryly statistical: "It will be noted," he wrote, "that less space is given in these pages to the events of war, and more to the affairs of peace" because statistics of sieges and battles are "of little value, and are apt to make us forget that the true glory of a nation lies after all, in orderly progress. Times of peace, the proverb says, have few historians; but this may be more the fault of the historians than of the times" (iii - iv). The result was a vivid and highly readable account of our past that shaped the historical understanding of generations of young Americans.

II *The "Despised Details" of Our Past*

Shortly after the reprinting of *Young Folks' History* in 1882, Higginson undertook a more ambitious work, *A Larger History of the United States of America* (1885). A massive study of the nation from the Viking exploration down to the close of Andrew Jackson's administration, the *Larger History* emphasized the theme of the discovery and settlement of America as "more important, more varied, more picturesque, and more absorbingly interesting than any historical subject offered by the world beside."[6]

In this claim for the picturesqueness of our past, Higginson differed from writers like Cooper, Hawthorne, and Lowell. Cooper had complained, in *Notions of the Americans* (1828), that in America there were "no annals for the historian." Hawthorne had deplored the panorama of our national life as "only a scene of 'common-place prosperity.'" And Lowell had called the early history of our country "essentially dry and unpoetic." Nevertheless, Higginson felt the necessity of taking up "just those despised details" in order to "see, by a fair test, whether any nation has better material to offer" (v - vi).

Working in collaboration with his young brother-in-law, the historian Edward Channing of Harvard, Higginson undertook "the lighter but not always easier task of the literary man to reduce these accumulations [of new knowledge] into compact shape, select what is most characteristic, and make the result readable" (vi). The result was successful. Higginson's overview of the exploratory voyages of the Vikings, Spanish, French, and English navigators, his account of the settlement of the colonies, and his review of the struggle for independence—leading to the formation of the federal republic and the administrations of the early presidents—is a model of sustained, highly interesting narrative.

The historical orientation of the *Larger History*, as Edelstein has shown, "reflected Bancroft's defense of Puritan society, Hildreth's allegiance to the Federalists, and his criticisms of Jefferson, and Parton's disdain for Jackson."[7] Higginson, for example, tried to correct the common misapprehension that the Puritans really sought religious liberty. For him, they sought only truth and—given their conception of religious truth—they exercised a fierce authority to exclude the heretical from plantations which they had founded to protect their beliefs. Higginson thus makes fully explicable the rationale behind Puritan treatment of the Indians, Quakers, Anabaptists, and, later, the reputed witches. Even so, he condemns as reprehensible the conduct of the Puritans, while noting that such persecutions were more widespread, virulent, and bloody in Europe.

Higginson conceded in the *Larger History* that "some Federalists were narrow-minded and some Jacksonians far-sighted,"[8] but, as a New Englander descended from Stephen Higginson of the Essex Junto, he condemned Jefferson's mercantile policies as embodying the prejudices of the Virginia planters. The Embargo of 1807, Higginson wrote, "brought ruin to so many households that it might well be at least doubted whether it brought good to any" (356). Yet when he came to summarize Jefferson's character and career, he was generally approbative:

Jefferson was a man full of thoughts and of studious purposes; trustful of the people, distrustful of the few; a generous friend, but a vehement and unscrupulous foe; not so much deliberately false as without a clear sense of truth; courageous for peace, but shrinking and vacillating in view of war; ignorant of his own limitations; as self-confident in financial and commercial matters, of which he knew little, as in respect to the principles of republican government, about which he showed more foresight than any man of his time. He may have underrated the dangers to which the nation might be exposed from ignorance and vice, but he never yielded, on the other hand, to the cowardice of culture; he never relaxed his faith in the permanence of popular government or in the high destiny of man. (358)

Andrew Jackson, on the other hand, he found to be "narrow, ignorant, violent, unreasonable" (432), and ruthless in his manipulation of the spoils system. Higginson recounts Old Hickory's rise to power through military victory over the Indian tribes and Great Britain, the major events of his administration, and his social troubles over the Peggy O'Neil affair, which had "an appreciable influence on the political history of the nation" (449). (It is worth remarking that, aside from the account of this scandal, one of the minor virtues of the *Larger History* is that Higginson lost few opportunities to emphasize the positive contribution to our history of American women.) Jackson's handling of the United States Bank and nullification issues is rehearsed, and the volume concludes—as we might have expected—with Garrison and the rise of abolitionism. In a dazzling act of reductionism, Higginson remarks that "for nearly half a century, the history of the nation was the history of the antislavery contest." The administration of Jackson, he concluded, would be

most remarkable, after all, . . . because of something that arose in spite of it—an agitation so far opposed to his wishes, in fact, that he wished for the passage of a law excluding antislavery publications from the mails. It was an agitation destined to draw new lines, to establish new standards, and create new reputations; and it is to be remembered that the Democratic President did not abhor it more, on the one side, than did his fiercest Federalist critics on the other. One of the ablest of them, William Sullivan, at the close of his "Familiar Letters on Public Characters," after exhausting language to depict the outrages committed by President Jackson, points out as equally objectionable the rising antislavery movement, and predicts that, if it has its full course, "even an Andrew Jackson may be a blessing." But of the wholly new series of events which were to date from this agitation neither Sullivan nor Jackson had so much as a glimpse. These pages may well close, for the present, with the dawn of that great revolution. (454 - 55)

Higginson never wrote a sequel to the *Larger History*, but a longer version of it was published in 1905—under the title of *History of the United States*. The longer version was completed in collaboration with William MacDonald, of Brown University, who revised the work and added a number of new chapters, submitting them for approval to the eighty-year-old Higginson. Such was the popularity of the *Larger History* and its successor that it satisfied at least the colonel's claim that those "despised details" of our early history did surpass in drama and excitement those of any other nation.

III   *Minor Works of Historical Prose*

In the aftermath of the Civil War, as I have observed, the nation developed anew an absorbing interest in the discovery and settlement of America. The war had aroused again that spirit of nationalism so common in the Revolutionary era. In consequence of this interest, Higginson published in 1877 *The Book of American*

Explorers, an account of the major navigators who discovered and explored America. Organized in fifteen chapters devoted to such mariners as Leif the Lucky, Columbus, Verrazano, de Soto, and Captain John Smith, Higginson presented in this volume an anthology of letters, journals, true relations, and other firsthand accounts of the explorations, in the effort to reveal to students "the charm of an original narrative." Though his principal task was selecting and editing the documents, he achieved here a highly readable selection illustrating a "great subject" which he felt to be "as interesting as Robinson Crusoe."[9] Similarly, *Travellers and Outlaws: Episodes in American History* (1889) undertook to illuminate our past by devoting attention to some of the lesser known figures whose histories had had a significant bearing on the national life. Believing that the "revelations of the reprobates"[10] could illuminate major events, Higginson told the stories of rebels like Captain Daniel Shays, Henry Tufts, and old Salem sea captains like Jonathan Haraden and Joseph Peabody. Less reprobate than mobile was William Ellery, whose story was told in "Revolutionary Congressman on Horseback." Higginson also narrated the histories of Denmark Vesey, Nat Turner, and other blacks and West Indians who had fomented insurrection against slavery. Although the sketches, like those in *The Book of American Explorers*, do not add up to a sustained history, they are successful narratives of great human interest and historical insight.

Of all of Higginson's historical prose, the *English History for American Readers* (1893) is perhaps the least significant. On this volume Higginson collaborated once more with Edward Channing, who seems to have amassed the materials while Higginson did the actual writing or revision. The key to the work is suggested in the title: it is an overview of British history in light of those events of particular interest to American readers—the development of the English as a race, the early struggles with the monarchy leading to the Magna Carta, the development of the constitutional system, the Puritan exodus, the rebellion against King Charles, and those political events which enlarged the liberties of Englishmen in the eighteenth and nineteenth centuries (parallel to like developments in America). Although Higginson tried "to avoid all unfair or one-sided judgments," his Americanism emerges in his discussion of Puritanism and the American Revolution, and in his doubtful claim, apropos of the Civil War, that the workingmen in England "recognized that the cause of the American Union was the cause of free labor the world over."[11] Intended to remedy American neglect of English history, the work had a simplicity and readability that sent it through three editions, although one reviewer was suspicious that, "like the earlier work of one of its authors, it is addressed to 'young folks.' "[12] The comment is not without its validity, for Higginson himself had elsewhere observed that "history, written as it should be, is all Swiss Family Robinson."[13]

The colonel's growing reputation as an historian led eventually to one further assignment in the service of Clio. Appointed the State Military and Naval Historian, Higginson was asked to compile the two-volume history of *Massachusetts in the Army and Navy during the War of 1861 - 1865* (1895 - 1896). Though his task for these volumes was principally editorial, his work provided a comprehensive overview of the state's contribution to the Union cause, the history of her regiments, their major battles and honors, a list of her officers, and the names of soldiers killed in battle. Never averse to giving credit where due, he included in this work a section entitled "Massachusetts Women in the War." To my knowledge, no contemporary historian of the Civil War so honored the contribution of women to the preservation of the Union.

IV   The Professional Historians' Estimate

What, finally, should be said about Higginson as an historian? First, it is worth emphasizing that Higginson never thought of himself as a professional historian. He always regarded himself as a man of letters who worked into readable shape stores of information researched and supplied by others. He had little interest in the newer "scientific" history emerging in the post - Civil War period, for he was shaped by the older Romantic historians who emphasized historical narrative as a literary art. Nevertheless, he was still inferior to accomplished writers like Bancroft, Parkman, Prescott, and Motley. The historian Edelstein has observed that Higginson "was one of those literary patricians of the era who pronounced the magisterial verdict of history upon men and events by making moral judgments. When Higginson's appointment to the Harvard history department was being considered by President Eliot, a retired Harvard professional historian recorded that 'all agreed to keep him at arm's length, but if he is to be taken any where it should be in the English Department, not Historical.' "[14]

Still, his historical prose merits considerable praise. For one thing, as a Cantabrigian descended from Puritans and Federalists who helped to shape the early nation, he felt intimately involved in the past, which he lovingly recreated. And as he had lived through and participated in the great events of the era of abolitionism, the Civil War, and Reconstruction, he had a firsthand knowledge of many of the participants and events he narrated. This element of personal interest tended to bias some of his conclusions, though he tried always to be equitable in describing national conflicts. Whether biased or not, his historical prose has a vividness and a satisfying element of felt significance. Moreover, he used original sources wherever possible in documenting his narratives. Though he sometimes quoted to excess, such quotation gave his interpretations a solid foundation in fact. In addition, he pioneered in the not inconsiderable field of juvenile history and theorized usefully about the demands of that discipline. Although his contribution as a scholar was negligible, his talent being popularization, Higginson was, as Howard W. Hintz has observed, "among the first of American historical writers to humanize and popularize historical study. He helped materially to lift it out of its ponderous, academic, and cataloguing state, and to inject life, color, dramatic interest, and stylistic grace into historical writing."[15] Although his histories have been altogether superseded by the more rigorous studies of those who came later, much of what he wrote retains an informative and compelling quality, thanks to the liveliness of his style.

CHAPTER 7

The Craft of Plutarch:
Higginson as a Biographer

I *Margaret Fuller*

AS a biographer, one of Higginson's merits is that he worked (whenever possible) from unpublished manuscript sources, thereby enlarging what had previously been known about his subjects. In this respect, *Margaret Fuller Ossoli*, published in 1890 in the "American Men of Letters" series, is one of his most satisfactory biographical performances. Margaret Fuller was an intimate of Emerson and a major intellectual force among the Concord Transcendentalists. Emerson, W. H. Channing, and James Freeman Clarke had told her story in the *Memoirs of Margaret Fuller Ossoli* (1852). Higginson thought this memoir to be useful in its time. But since Margaret Fuller had been born and bred in the same town as he, since she had been a friend of his older sisters and he a playmate of her younger brothers, and since her sister and niece had lived with him after her death, he brought to his task unusual sympathy, for he confessed that she had "a more immediate intellectual influence" on him than anyone except Emerson and Theodore Parker.[1]

In consequence of his knowledge of her life and work, Higginson's biography superseded both the *Memoirs* and Julia Ward Howe's brief biography, *Margaret Fuller (Marchesa) Ossoli* (1883). Margaret Fuller is here revealed through much hitherto unpublished manuscript material, including the five volumes of material touching her life kept by the family: her letters to Emerson, Frederick H. Hedge, A. G. Green, George T. Davis, and W. H. Channing; her diary of 1844; her travel diary in England and Scotland (which Higginson owned); the manuscript diary of Bronson Alcott; and her correspondence with her husband, in a transla-

111

tion made for him by Elizabeth Hoar. To these original unpublished documents Higginson brought a wealth of information
solicited from friends in Cambridge and Boston, and the insight of
many books, published after her death, about the period of
Transcendentalism.

The book is a conventional biography in that Higginson traces
Margaret Fuller's hereditary traits and family background, her
girlhood at Cambridge, her country life at Groton, and her early
career teaching in Boston and Providence. All of this background he
considered an apprenticeship for her central role in the
Transcendental movement in Boston and Concord. He describes
the novelty of her consciousness-raising "conversations" with
women in Boston and Cambridge, the founding of the Transcendental Club, and her editorship (during the first two years) of
the *Dial*, the major periodical of Transcendental thought. He
repudiates the claim that she was the model for Zenobia in
Hawthorne's *The Blithedale Romance*. And he reviews, sym-
pathetically, her published books, including her *Correspondence
with Goethe* (1839), *Correspondence with Fraülein Günderode and
Bettine von Arnim* (1842), *Woman in the Nineteenth Century*
(1844), and *Papers on Literature and Art* (1846). He traces in detail
her journalistic life in New York, as a correspondent for Horace
Greeley's *Tribune*, and follows her to Europe, where she secretly
married the revolutionary Marquis Ossoli. He deals in a touching
way with the love letters between Margaret Fuller and her husband
during the invasion and occupation of Rome; he records the birth of
their son; and he recounts their affecting death in a shipwreck off
Fire Island, on their return voyage to the United States.

The thesis of his biography is that Margaret Fuller was an activist, not—as she had been presented in the *Memoirs*—a
Transcendental dreamer given to airy, impractical schemes. Higginson commended her as a woman intellectual of the first order.
"Coming in contact, as she did, with some of the strongest men of
her time; first the Boston Transcendentalists; then Horace Greeley
in New York; then Mazzini in Italy: she was still her own mis-
tress. . . . This showed not merely a strong nature—for strength
alone does not secure independence—but a rich and wise one." He
notes that she was sometimes "confused, rambling, sometimes high-
flown," but she offered "no paradoxes so startling as some of Emerson's, and is incomparably smoother and clearer than Alcott" (284 -
85). Though Higginson felt that she suffered from "an exuberance

of mental activity," which she never learned to control because she died so young, he felt that *Woman in the Nineteenth Century* was a major document in the feminist crusade and that *Papers on Literature and Art* earned her "a very high place among American prose-writers" (288).

Higginson believed that Margaret Fuller excelled her Transcendental contemporaries in two especial gifts. One was her " 'lyric glimpses,' or the power of putting a high thought into a sentence" (288). The other was her talent, as it seemed to Higginson, as "the best literary critic whom America has yet seen" (290). He regarded her paper on Goethe in the *Dial,* her paper on Mackintosh, and her essay "Modern British Poets" to be superlative instances of practical Transcendental criticism.

Higginson felt especially obliged to explain away her criticisms of Lowell and Longfellow. Looking back after fifty years, it seemed to him that "she did less than justice to them both," though her remarks were not dictated by personal rancor. Of Longfellow she complained, "He has no style of his own, growing out of his own experiences and observations of nature. Nature with him, whether human or external, is always seen through the windows of literature. There are in his poems sweet and tender passages descriptive of his personal feelings, but very few showing him as an observer, at first hand, of the passions within, or the landscape without" (294). With Lowell she was even blunter. She claimed that he was "absolutely wanting in the true spirit and tone of poesy," and that "his interest in the moral questions of the day" had "supplied the want of vitality in himself." She claimed that his "great facility at versification" had enabled him "to fill the ear with a copious stream of pleasant sound. But his verse is stereotyped; his thought sounds no depth, and posterity will not remember him" (297). Viewed from the perspective of the 1890s, when Longfellow and Lowell were beloved Brahmins recited in every schoolroom, Margaret Fuller's opinions seemed to Higginson to have been oddly ungenerous. Almost a century later, however, how accurate seem her conclusions about these two popular New England poets. Nevertheless, friend of Lowell and student of Longfellow, Higginson was blind to the acuity of her judgment, though he acknowledged its force.

Higginson believed, finally, that it was Margaret Fuller who had been unfairly treated by her New England contemporaries. Emerson, with his "cool and tranquil temperament," did not always do "quite justice to the ardent nature that flung itself against him";

and he held that "her other biographers have sometimes been too much influenced by their own point of contact with her to see that the self-culture which brought her to them was by no means the whole of her aim" (300). He absolved her of the charge of vanity and self-absorption. If she was not "universally beloved," Higginson found the reason to be in her wAnt of tact, in her plainspoken truthfulness. And if she was "strict and unflinching in her judgments of other people," it was for Higginson because "she was so, above all, in dealing with herself" (306). Her letters and diaries made plain to Higginson a yearning desire not merely to know but to do, and he stressed the extent to which she was willing to criticize even Emerson himself for his "half-cloistered life at Concord" (310). For Higginson she was "the most cultivated American woman of her day." Hers was a triumphant rather than a sad life, despite her father's stern educational theories, her prolonged illness, her poverty, and her disappointments. She had the three great qualities which Browning called for—"life and love and Italy." "She shared in great deeds, she was the counselor of great men, she had a husband who was a lover, and she had a child. They loved each other in their lives, and in their death they were not divided." (314). For Higginson these qualities and talents, these energies and accomplishments, added up to a remarkable life.

II *Longfellow*

Less satisfactory, it seems to me, is Higginson's biography *Henry Wadsworth Longfellow* (1902), also published in the "American Men of Letters" series. Though Higginson had access to Longfellow's correspondence with his first wife, and made use of unpublished materials touching Longfellow's teaching career at Harvard, this life is unoriginal and furnishes no essential view not implied in the life earlier written by the poet's brother, Samuel Longfellow. Nevertheless, Higginson's biography dutifully recounts the birth, childhood, and youth of the poet, his first flights at authorship, his commitment to a life of literature, his various visits to Europe, his two marriages, his appointment at Bowdoin and at Harvard as a professor of modern languages and literature, and his development and achievement as a poet and translator. Higginson was at great pains to answer the question of whether Longfellow was a classic. Writing in 1902, of course, Higginson had every reason to believe that the poet's immortality was assured. Indeed, who could have guessed at the turn of the century that the author of "Evangeline," "Hiawatha," "Hyperion," "Voices of the Night," and "Christus"—the poet who seemed to be the equal of Tennyson, and whose bust had been installed in the Poet's Corner in Westminster Abbey—would be so nearly forgotten a mere seventy-five years later. These failures of prophecy aside, Higginson found "the great literary lesson of Longfellow's life" in the fact that he was "the first among American poets to create for himself a world-wide fame" and that he was "guided from youth to age by a strong national feeling, or at any rate by the desire to stand for the life and the associations by which he was habitually surrounded."[2]

Higginson's life of Longfellow thus contradicts the charge, often made against the poet, that he was mesmerized by Europe and the cultural tradition of the Old World. Higginson quotes with approval the "American feeling" of Longfellow's early commencement oration, "Our Native Writers," where the poet praised the "spirit and a love of literature" that were "springing up in the shadow of our free political institutions" (31). Higginson felt "Evangeline," "The Courtship of Miles Standish," "Hiawatha," and "The Wayside Inn" to be signal illustrations of the Americanness of the poet. Yet Longfellow was also the author of "Nuremberg," *The Belfry of Bruges*, and other works reflecting the glories of European culture. In *Kavanagh* (1849), he had questioned the value of nationalism in literature, concluding that "all that is best in the great poets of all countries is not what is national in them, but what is universal." Longfellow had little sympathy with Emerson's call, in "The American Scholar," for a rejection of "the courtly Muses of Europe." As Longfellow told a friend in 1844, "A national literature is the expression of national character and thought; and as our character and modes of thought do not differ essentially from those of England, our literature cannot" (263). Though Higginson had some trouble with the evidence of national feeling, he concluded that "Longfellow rendered a service only secondary [to Emerson, who "freed" American literature], in enriching and refining it and giving it a cosmopolitan culture, and an unquestioned standing in the literary courts of the civilized world" (262).

III *Whittier*

Higginson's biography *John Greenleaf Whittier* (1902), written for the "English Men of Letters" series, is of a piece with the

literary biographies just discussed. Written out of Higginson's intimate knowledge of the Quaker poet, and indebted to Pickard's
authorized life, this biography recounts the poet's childhood and
schooling, his youthful political passions, his enlistment in the
abolitionist cause, and Whittier's personal, social, and literary
qualities. Higginson found Whittier to be an utter contrast to
Longfellow:

> Longfellow was the most widely traveled author of the Boston circle,
> Whittier the least so; Longfellow spoke a variety of languages, Whittier
> only his own; Longfellow had whatever the American college of his time
> could give him, Whittier had none of it; Longfellow had the habits of a
> man of the world, Whittier those of a recluse; Longfellow touched reform
> but lightly, Whittier was essentially imbued with it; Longfellow had
> children and grandchildren, while Whittier led a single life. Yet in certain
> gifts, apart from poetic quality, they were alike; both being modest, serene,
> unselfish, brave, industrious, and generous. They either shared or made up
> between them, the highest and most estimable qualities that mark poet or
> man.[3]

It was therefore no surprise to Higginson that, among at least
English readers, Longfellow was the most popular of American
poets, Whittier standing second.

As befits a biographical study, Higginson's emphasis is on the
record of Whittier's life and his personal qualities. Here, as
everywhere, Higginson emphasizes the "ideal" qualities and virtues
of the man—his generosity, his sense of humor, his philanthropy,
his service in behalf of social reform. Clearly Higginson had
moderate enthusiasm for Whittier as a poet, though he points ad-
miringly to "Snow-Bound," "The Barefoot Boy," "The External
Goodness," "Massachusetts to Virginia," "My Soul and I,"
"Ichabod," and "Proem." These poems demonstrate, for Higginson, that Whittier was "the distinctively American poet of familiar
life" (151), whose "imperfections were those of his time and
class"—a lack of compression, a "fatal fluency" (153). But he conceded that the poems win us "by the sincerity and ingenuousness of
his verse, rooted in the soil and nature as the fern and wildrose of
the wayside" (154 - 55).

Higginson felt Whittier's defects to be manifest—an ignorance of
music; a weakness for the overlong poem, "laden with a superfluous
moral," tending to ennui; oddities of mispronunciation; and doubtful grammar. We cannot quarrel with these criticisms of Whittier as

a poet, but Higginson's comments on Whittier's rhymes are disconcerting. Higginson thought Whittier's rhymes not as bad as those of Elizabeth Barrett Browning. But he objected to such rhymes as *worn* and *turn*, *joins* and *pines*, *faults* and *revolts*, *flood* and *Hood*, *even* and *Devon*, *heaven* and *forgiven*, *pearl* and *marl*, *scamper* and *Hampshire*. None of these, in the abstract, is objectionable; nor in context does Whittier's saying it slant offend the modern reader. But Higginson's literary education predisposed him to require perfect rhymes of the poet. And even in the presence of Emily Dickinson, the first poetic genius of the oblique rhyme, Higginson was unable to give full sympathy.

Yet Whittier, for Higginson, survived his defects. He called Whittier the "leading bard of the greatest moral movement of the Age," abolition. Antislavery agitation gave Whittier "a training in directness, simplicity, genuineness; it taught him to shorten his sword and to produce strong effects by common means." Higginson concluded that abolitionism "made him permanently high-minded also." And—in a remark that reveals the fundamental moral orientation of all of the Brahmin critics—Higginson praised the way that the antislavery crusade placed Whittier, "as he himself always said, above the temptations of a merely literary career" (160).

IV Harvard Memorial Biographies

After the war, Higginson consented, as he told his army surgeon, Dr. Rogers, "to edit the memorial volumes containing the lives of those Harvard boys who have died in the war—it will take me a year almost."[4] Although this was principally an editorial project, the colonel was inundated with letters and memoirs of the dead soldiers; he conducted many interviews with friends and relatives of the slain; and, of the ninety-five essays, he wound up writing the lives of twelve of the young men. The result was *Harvard Memorial Biographies* (1866), in two volumes. Reviewing the tragic sacrifice of these men, Higginson commended their devotion to the nation, noting that many of them had been descended from colonial and Revolutionary patriots. He rejected the charge of the "supposed torpor or alienation prevailing among cultivated Americans," noting that higher education had admirably instilled in them a sense of their patriotic responsibility: "I do not see how any one can read these memoirs," he wrote, "without being left with fresh confidence in our institutions, in the American people, and indeed in human nature itself."[5] They were, as Lowell put it in his "Commemoration Ode," Harvard's "wisest scholars, those who understood / The deeper teaching of her mystic tome, / And offered their fresh lives to make it good."

V *Francis Higginson*

Although his lives of nineteenth-century writers are more satisfying because he knew the men and women he wrote about, we cannot leave this section on Higginson the biographer without noticing his two other biographies—the *Life of Francis Higginson* (1891) and *Life and Times of Stephen Higginson* (1907). The former, written for the "Makers of America" series, is a portrait of the first minister in the Massachusetts Bay Colony. Much of the book is composed of extracts from *Magnalia Christi Americana*, where Cotton Mather tells "the story of that worthy man; who, when 't is considered that he crossed the *sea* with a renowned *colony*, and that having seen an *old world* in *Europe*, where a flood of iniquity and calamity carried all before it, he also saw a *new world* in *America*; where he appears the first in a catalogue of heroes, and where he and his people were admitted into the *covenant* of God; whereupon a hedge of *piety* and *sanctity* continued about *that* people as long as *he* lived; may therefore be called the *Noah* or *Janus* of *New England*. This was Mr. *Francis Higginson*."[6]

Reviewing the history of that first migration to New England, Mather was right to list Francis Higginson as "the first in a catalogue of heroes." A Puritan divine educated at Jesus College, with a ministry in Leicester, Higginson became discontented with the corruptions in the Church of England and accepted the call to found a plantation of the Church of Christ in New England. He was not a Separatist, but he went to America "to practise the positive part of church reformation, and propagate the gospel in America" (29).

Wentworth Higginson recounts the planning of the Puritan expedition, the sea voyage aboard the *Mayflower* and other ships, the "true relations" sent back to England, and the settlement at Nahum-kek, which Higginson renamed Salem. Preaching on the text of Matthew 12:7, "What went you out into the wilderness to see?", the Reverend Mr. Higginson "minded the people of the *design,* whereupon this plantation was erected, namely religion: and of the streights, wants, and various *trials,* which in a *wilderness* they must look to meet withal; and of the need which there was for them to evidence the *uprightness* of their hearts, in the end of their coming hither" (129). Higginson wrote the covenant by which those settlers bound themselves to the authority of God, their governors, and ministers—a significant document in early American social theory. And he wrote one of the most factual and informative descriptions of the first New World experience—*New Englands Plantation* (1630). Yet Francis Higginson suffered consumption, and like many of the other immigrants, he may have contracted scurvy from the long voyage and the privations ashore. The Puritans landed in May 1629; in September 1630 Francis Higginson died at the age of forty-three. He had eight children, of whom the American branch was descended from his son John, who lived to the age of ninety-two—through, that is, the Quaker persecutions and the great witchcraft trials. Wentworth Higginson remarks that John characterized the Quaker's Inner Light as "a stinking vapor from hell" and approved the sentence of Thomas Maule (alluded to in Hawthorne's *The House of the Seven Gables*), to be whipped ten stripes for saying that "Mr. Higginson preached lies, and his doctrine was the doctrine of devils." Yet old John Higginson protested against both the witchcraft delusion and African slavery, testifying in behalf of a neighbor woman charged with witchcraft, and giving moral encouragement to Samuel Sewall for writing the antislavery pamphlet *The Selling of Joseph*. John Higginson wrote the preface to Mather's *Magnalia Christi Americana* and testified to the truth of Mather's account from personal knowledge, since "now above sixty-eight years in New England . . . *I have seen all that the Lord* hath done for his people . . ." (146).

From Francis and John Higginson descended all the members of the family of that name, as well as, on the distaff side, many conspicuous New England leaders (George Cabot, John Lowell), generals (William Tecumseh Sherman), several senators (Evarts, Hoar, and John Sherman), many congressmen (Andrew, Lodge, Sherman Hoar), many lawyers, clergymen, physicians, authors, scholars, and soldiers.[7] One of the most important of these descendants of the Noah who came hitherward in the ark of religious truth was Stephen Higginson.

VI *Stephen Higginson*

In *Life and Times of Stephen Higginson*, Wentworth told the story of his grandfather, a great patriot of the American Revolution. He had seen him only once, in 1828, when, as a boy of five, his parents had taken him out to Brookline to the ancient Federalist's estate. Wentworth could remember him only as "an aged man wearing small-clothes such as I had never seen my father wear, and walking with an old-fashioned cane." For Wentworth, as for W. H. Channing, the old man, in his powdered queue, ruffled wristbands, silk knee stockings, and buckled shoes, was "the type of all that was most ancient and venerable."[8] He was a living embodiment of the American Revolution.

Stephen Higginson was great-great-grandson of the original Puritan founder, Francis Higginson. Wentworth's grandfather, born in 1743, was a seaman, supercargo, and captain whose first publicity came when he was summoned before a committee of the House of Commons in 1771 to be interrogated by Edmund Burke and others on the effect of new bills to restrict the New England fisheries. "On his return to this country, he was vehemently attacked at Marblehead, and even brought before court on charge of traitorous conduct, but had fortunately kept a copy of his precise answers, and won much applause when he produced them" (21 - 22).

Stephen Higginson pursued maritime commerce until the Revolution; thereupon he ventured into privateering. Afterwards, he was a staunch Federalist and a member of the "Essex Junto," which lost out to Jefferson and his followers in the political struggles of the early Republic. Elected to the Continental Congress in 1782, he served briefly in a legislative body hamstrung by its lack of established legal authority. The problems with the fledgling Congress led Hamilton to call for a convention of the states in Annapolis, which Higginson attended, for the purpose of rendering "the Constitution of the Federal Government adequate to the exigencies of the Union" (68). This convention was followed in 1787 by the Constitutional Convention, which proposed our present form of government.

In the aftermath of the Revolution, many of the common people were impoverished, paper currency was nearly valueless, debts had accumulated, and taxes were high. In 1786, mobs in western Massachusetts led by Daniel Shays rioted, and the spectre of anarchy threatened to destroy the new federal government. When Shays' Rebellion erupted, Higginson and others petitioned the governor to suppress the mobs: "in our situation, without Energy and without any Funds beside what may be drawn from the people by Taxes, it is a serious and important Question, whether our Government may not yet get unhinged, and a revolution take place, before the Cure be effected, and the people at large discover, that to secure their liberties and the great bulk of their property a certain portion of the latter must be parted with. We appear to be verging fast to a Crisis" (85). The governor and the council had warrants issued for the arrest of Shays and his ringleaders. And it appears that Wentworth's grandfather Stephen was second in command of the troop that rode into backcountry Massachusetts to crush the rebellion.

Wentworth took satisfaction in noting that Stephen Higginson "clearly . . . saw, what many others did not, that the disturbances under Shays were not only, in his phrase, 'much more deeply rooted' than was apprehended, but that they had at least the advantage of furnishing the very strongest argument in favor of a more efficient general government than a mere confederacy could ever furnish" (102). Stephen Higginson told General Knox that "as all the States are at least equally exposed with this to such Commotions, and none of them are capable of the exertions we have made, they will have reason to fear the worst consequences to themselves, unless the Union shall have force enough to give the same effectual aid in a like case. Those who now have the administration of Government in the several States and for the Union, must seize every opportunity to increase its energy and stability; or Insurgents will soon rise up, and take the reins from them" (104). Realizing the state of near anarchy because "the seeds [of rebellion] yet remain in the soil," Higginson reiterated his plea to "Mr. Maddison" and others of "the Idea of a special Convention for the purpose of revising the Confederation and increasing the powers of the Union" (112). Wentworth recounts his grandfather's argument that "powers delineated on paper cannot alone be sufficient, the Union must not only have the right to make Laws and requisitions, but it must have the power also of compelling obedience thereto, otherwise our federal Constitution will be a mere dead letter" (112 - 13). Higginson recommended a federal Constitution "empowered to perfect the system, and give it immediate operation, if nine states in the Convention shall agree to it" (114). Stephen Higginson was thus apparently the first to suggest—and this gave his grandson supreme satisfaction—"the precise method by which the United States Constitution was finally established and confederation . . . came to an end" (115).

Reverting afterwards to mercantile life, Higginson remained a successful merchant until 1812, when Jefferson's Embargo ruined him. Nevertheless, Wentworth had reason to be proud of his grand-father, for it was he who had said in 1790: "The public mind, to judge from this part of the Union, has kept pace with the times; and has been prepared, with wonderful success and facility, for new Events. There seems to be a general conviction, that the Union must be supported, as the alone Source of national Security; and that every burthen necessary to the Object must be cheerfully bourne" (155). This biography served a useful service in highlighting the career of an important patriot who stood, nevertheless, at the periphery of the great events of the Revolutionary era. Compared with Washington, Jefferson, or Adams, he is a minor figure—and one, moreover, whose federalism marked him for later political defeat. But however minor, he was one of a number of those whose joint efforts overthrew a tyrannical monarchy and instituted the constitutional system under which we still live.

VII   Brief Lives

Aside from the full-length biographies of literary figures like Whittier, Longfellow, and Margaret Fuller, Higginson wrote more than a score of biographical essays on other writers and public figures. Chiefly published in the *Atlantic*, the *Nation*, and *Century Magazine*, many of these brief lives were collected and reprinted in volume two of the collected writings under the title *Contemporaries* (1900). Aside from "the natural instinct of preserving one's own work," he collected them "because a group of such personal delineations has some increase of value when recognized as proceeding from one mind, and thus expressing the same general point of view." All of them, except the narrative of his visit to Captain John Brown's household, were revised for the book publication in the light of "the development of new facts or by the reconsideration of opinions"; the narrative of the Brown visit was left untouched, "as the only mode of preserving the precise atmosphere of the thrilling period when it was originally written."[9]

Contemporaries presents a great many vignettes of leading literary figures of Higginson's time—Emerson, Alcott, Whittier, Whitman, Lanier, Helen Hunt Jackson—as well as miscellaneous essays like "The Eccentricities of Reformers" and "The Road to England." The essays on literary figures, while full of biographical notation and personal reminiscence, also aspire to criticism; a consideration of them is therefore deferred until chapter eight, where Higginson's criticism is discussed. Setting aside these essays, the most important group of these brief lives deals with the leading antislavery reformers during the antebellum years. The chief of these is memorialized in "William Lloyd Garrison."

For Higginson, Garrison was the figure at the "living centre of a remarkable group of men who have had no equals among us, in certain moral attributes, since the Revolutionary period and perhaps not then" (244). Garrison was a nonresistant and a pacifist, yet Higginson counted himself among his followers. Firm, well-built, grave, and tireless in his abolitionism, Garrision was scathing in his invective, "but as it was almost always mainly scriptural, it did not carry an impression of personal anger, but simply seemed like a newly discovered chapter of Ezekiel" (246).

Garrison and his followers broke with the less pacific opponents to slavery and alienated other abolitionists who scrupled not at the Sabbath Question and yet believed in the vote—Whittier, Lundy, Goodell, James G. Birney, and the Grimké sisters. For them, Garrison came to seem arrogant, imperious, and dictatorial, Sarah Grimké testifying that Garrison and his followers "wanted us to live out William Lloyd Garrison, not the convictions of our own souls; entirely unaware that they were exhibiting, in the high places of moral reform, the genuine spirit of slaveholding, by wishing to curtail the sacred privilege of conscience" (250 - 51).

Yet despite the internal bickering among the abolitionists, the important point for Garrison and Higginson was that they all should agree on "the root of the matter." Thus Garrison's most vituperative discourse, in *The Liberator* and elsewhere, was reserved for the "peculiar institution" and the Southern slaveholders. "For myself, I hold no fellowship with slaveowner," he had written. "I will not make a truce with them even for a single hour. I blush for them as countrymen. I *know* that they are not *Christian;* and the higher they raise their professions of patriotism or piety, the stronger is my detestation of their hypocrisy. They are dishonest and cruel,—and God and the angels and devils of the universe know that *they are without excuse*" (253).

One may doubt that Higginson, as a Christian minister in the 1850s, sympathized too deeply with this wholesale condemnation. Afterwards, it was clear—at least to Higginson—that many Southerners had been exempt from Garrison's sweeping charge. The facts of ignorance, heredity, and environment, Higginson held, mitigated in some degree the sins of the slaveholder. Moreover, in view of the fact that in South Carolina, Georgia, Alabama, and Mississippi "a man becoming heir to human property was absolutely prohibited from emancipating it except by a special authority of the legislature, a permission usually impossible to get" (254), Garrison's claim obviously went too far. Yet, while "not faultless," Garrison "kept far higher laws than he broke," Higginson concluded, and in leading the abolitionist cause he achieved a secure fame, recognized in "the chorus of affectionate congratulations that marked his closing days" (256).

In "Wendell Phillips" Higginson paid tribute to another of his abolitionist contemporaries. He was on familiar ground with Phillips, for the Boston orator's background was rather like Higginson's. Phillips was a man of wealth and aristocratic reputation, but these he commendably sacrificed to the cause. The keynote of Phillips's success was his oratory. So effective were his speeches in Boston that Higginson and his confederates were often required to serve as Phillips's bodyguard at public meetings, where the proslavery mobs were constantly threatening bodily harm.

Higginson felt some disappointment in Phillips's conduct after the emancipation of the slaves, for "he simply reverted" to "that career of cultivated leisure from which the anti-slavery movement had wrenched him for forty years" (275). Though temperance, labor, and woman's suffrage might have used his talents, Phillips became "a critic of music, a frequenter of the theatres." Yet Phillips "belonged to the heroic type." His death, in 1884, closed for Higginson "one great chapter of American history" (278 - 79).

Little need be said about the chapters devoted to Lydia Maria Child, the "American Fanny Burney," whose *Anti-Slavery Standard* and *Letters from New York* won her "that warmth of sympathy, that mingled gratitude of intellect and heart which men give to those who have faithfully served their day and generation" (141); or to Samuel Gridley Howe, one of the "Secret Six" who "had quite made up their minds to fight" (296); or to Senator Charles Sumner, who in congressional activity was "unequaled among the Americans of his generation" (286). Nor need we linger over his sketches of the minor contemporaries he thought notable—John Holmes (the Autocrat's brother), Thaddeus William Harris (the naturalist), or Mrs. Hawthorne. We need only note that these brief biographies had the value of firsthand knowledge and reflect, on the whole, sympathetic understanding. If his treatment of like-minded New

Englanders ran to encomium, while those differing from himself merited less sympathy; if they lack the researched understanding of the longer biographies, while capitalizing on whatever impressions and recollections came to mind, they give us, as Mme Blanc once remarked, "the impression of entering into a closer intimacy"; they show us his contemporaries "as he himself knew them, as neighbors and friends"; and if, as is sometimes the case, "he tells us nothing fresh about them," [10] he still performed a useful service in putting on record his recollection of their contribution to American life.

CHAPTER 8

The Craft of Criticism:
Higginson on American Writing

A S the preceding chapters have tried to make clear, Wentworth Higginson was an unusually versatile writer who tried his hand (if he did not always succeed) at writing poetry, fiction, history, and the literature of political and social argument. Most of his energies, however, went into biography and literary criticism, forms sometimes almost indistinguishable, as they tend to shade into one another through personal reminiscence and anecdote. Reared in a literary culture in Cambridge, educated by Emerson, Thoreau, and Whittier, and the Brahmin luminaries Lowell, Holmes, and Longfellow, Higginson loved literature and felt a deep need to discourse about it in lectures, essays, and longer biographical studies.

Although he never formulated a coherent literary aesthetic, nevertheless some general principles may be inferred from his work as a practicing critic. In "Literature As an Art" (1867), "Youth and the Literary Life" (1892), and "Literature As a Pursuit" (1905), Higginson celebrated and defended, with missionary fervor, the life devoted to reading and writing. That life sharpened one's understanding, put one in touch with great ideas, refined the powers of expression, and ennobled the spirit. In essence, literature for him meant style, and style meant thoroughness of preparation, simplicity, freshness, self-restraint, unity of structure, and rigorous attention to revision. The well-formed style—especially in conjunction with the themes of social liberalism and spiritual idealism—always elicited from him the highest praise. Known himself as a distinguished stylist, Higginson called for richness of ornament, elegant metaphor, and rhetorical grace in prose literature. In the 1870s, when the new science of Darwin, Tyndall, and Huxley was revolutionizing English education, Higginson defended the older

concept of education based on languages and literature. Abhorring
the spreading plain style of scientific denotation, he wrote: "It is for
literature, after all, that I plead; not for this or that body of
literature [like the Classics]. Welcoming science, I only deprecate
the exclusive adoption of the scientific style."[1] Nevertheless, he is
not an aesthetic critic; criticism for him was always founded on
moral and social ideals.

I *General Principles of Criticism*

Studies in History and Letters (1900), volume five of the
collected writings, is a miscellany of essays Higginson had composed between 1858 and 1891. Many had been previously published
in *Atlantic Essays* (1871). Only a few deal with genuine historical
subjects;[2] most of them discourse on literary issues like "Sappho,"
"The Greek Goddesses," and "A Contemporaneous Posterity." A
number of them, however, touch on deeper matters affecting his
conception of the literary situation in the later nineteenth century
and thus deserve fuller attention.

In one of these, "The Literary Pendulum," Higginson expressed
dissatisfaction with the vagaries of mere taste in literature, the fluc-
tuation of reputations on the literary stock market, and the un-
trustworthiness of fads in literature. He felt that, "so strong has
been the recent swing of the pendulum in favor of what is called
realism in fiction, it is very possible that if Hawthorne's 'Twice-told
Tales' were to appear for the first time tomorrow they would attract
no more attention than they did more than fifty years ago."[3] Yet
Hawthorne was preeminently, for Higginson, a great artist whose
fame would survive the rise of Realism. Consequently, he adjured
his readers not to be a slave to the pendulum of taste. He urged a
longer perspective, a wider point of view, based on high-minded
ideals like the democratic principle of respect for the individual.
Translated into art, such ideals offered a surer basis for assessing the
worth of literature.

Despite his call for a high-minded criticism, which transcended
an interest in the merely ephemeral, Higginson did not care for
cosmopolitanism in art. In "A Cosmopolitan Standard," the colonel
argued against a wider standard than the national because
"cosmopolitanism" in literature had become simply another name
for deference to European values. Until the cosmopolitan standard
in politics and art included "the judgment of the New World on the

Old, as much as that of the Old World on the New" (306), the term
was useless. With an eye to Henry James and Matthew Arnold, he
observed that "we shall not prepare ourselves for a cosmopolitan
standard by ignoring our own great names or undervaluing the
literary tradition that has produced them" (309).

A like point of view is expressed in "Do We Need a Literary Centre?" Deploring the concentration of writing talent in a literary
capital, Higginson observed that an American literature would
necessarily have to proceed from many geographical sources, and he
saluted the signs of genius arising in the various regions of the local
colorists. Henry James, in *Hawthorne* (1879), had complained of
our provincialism, claiming that even Hawthorne's genius was sti-
fled by the aridity of aesthetic culture in Massachusetts, and James
had written *Roderick Hudson* more or less to document the poverty,
for the artist, of American life. But if James pitied Hawthorne "for
dwelling amid the narrowing influence of a Concord atmosphere,"
Higginson could not be perturbed. If "those influences gave us
'The Scarlet Letter' and Emerson's 'Essays,' does it not seem a
pity," he asked, "that we cannot extend the same local atmosphere,
as President Lincoln proposed to do with Grant's whiskey, to some
of our other generals?" (272).

These patriotic views are given fuller definition in a comparable
essay, "The New World and the New Book." There the language of
the Declaration of Independence is advanced as the touchstone of
values for an American literature, for that stirring document had
declared "the essential dignity and value of the individual man"
(246), which must be the basis for any democratic art. There is, he
pointed out, little upward social mobility in the fiction of Austen or
Scott because the social order generally obstructed rising in the
social scale. Yet American life was rich in social possibilities, and
Higginson held it the task of our literature to reflect and affirm the
openness of our social institutions. Higginson was not really a friend
of Realism in fiction, which had been controversially espoused by
Howells, James, De Forest, and other young American writers. It
lacked the element of the Ideal. But he came to think that works
like *The Rise of Silas Lapham, Annie Kilburn,* and *A Hazard of
New Fortunes* effectively presented "the dignity and importance of
the individual man." Thus he concluded that it was with the
egalitarian Howells and "with the school he represents that the
hope of American literature just now rests" (254).

What was, for Higginson, this hope for American literature and how should it be realized? These questions are effectively answered in perhaps the most important of the essays in *Studies in History and Letters*, "Americanism in Literature." It identifies Higginson as a member of what in our literary history has been called the party of hope, or the party of progress, as opposed to the party of the past. If Longfellow had perpetuated the influence of Europe on the American scene and Hawthorne had dealt with how the past impinges on the present, Higginson advocated "an attitude not necessarily connected with culture nor with the absence of culture, but with the consciousness of a new impulse given to all human progress" (220).

The American idea meant for Higginson "the faith that national self-government is not a chimera, but that, with whatever inconsistencies and drawbacks, we are steadily establishing it here. It includes the faith that to this good thing all other good things must in time be added" (221). The chief thing to be added, of course, was an American culture, a richer literary culture, a civilization in the European sense. Given his faith in our potentialities, he believed that a nation of grand prairies and Pacific slopes could be confident that in due time it would become fully civilized.

Much of "Americanism in Literature" concerns the first question of the development of the American character. Slow in taking form, we yet are aiming, he held, at "something better than our English fathers." The Civil War had marked a great advance in the formation of a national character, for it "subordinated local distinctions, cleared us our chief shame," and gave us "the pride of a common career" (222-23). In view of that great stride forward, he did not believe that immigration—the influx of southern Europeans, Chinese, Jews, and other minorities then thought undesirable—constituted a real obstacle to the development of a national identity. He had no sympathy with the "unguarded gates" fear. When all the ingredients in the great national pot should have melted, Americanism in literature would become a reality.

"Americanism in Literature" thus carried forward the torch raised by Emerson in "The American Scholar" in that it urged America to become civilized "not by any conscious effort, such as implies attitudinizing and constraint, but by simply accepting our own life" (223-24). Originality, he felt, would come with a fresh perspective on human experience—*that* perspective given by our novel social order—and through an attentive use of the materials of American life lying at hand—such as Emerson had foreshadowed with the humble-bee, the Rhodora, and the wood-thrush—in preference to the English daisy, the skylark, and the nightingale. "The truly cosmopolitan writer," he argued, "is not he who carefully denudes his work of everything occasional and temporary, but he who makes his local coloring forever classic through the fascination of the dream it tells. Reason, imagination, passion, are universal," he observed, "but sky, climate, costume, and even type of human character, belong to some one alone till they find an artist potent enough to stamp their associations on the memory of all the world." Higginson did not care whether the artist's work be "picture or symphony, legend or lyric," for "the spirit of the execution is all in all" (225).

Given Higginson's own career as a man of letters, one of his strangest criticisms of American literature is his claim that we yet lack distinction because of the miscellaneousness of our literary life. "The popular preacher becomes a novelist; the editor turns his paste-pot and scissors to the compilation of a history; the same man must be poet, wit, philanthropist, and genealogist" (226). In consequence, "the tone of our national literature . . . suffers. There is nothing in American life that can make concentration cease to be a virtue. Let a man choose his pursuit, and make all else count for recreation only." This is a telling criticism. Yet coming from a minister-reformer-soldier-editor-poet-novelist-critic, the remark is extraordinary. Apparently Higginson did not really understand Goethe's warning about the dissipation of one's powers through diverse activity, for there is no evidence in the essay, and very little in his life, to suggest that he ever applied such wisdom to his own work. In fact, the essay mitigates "desultory activity" by citing the advantage that "it makes men look in a variety of directions for a standard" (227).

Americanism in literature, in any event, would necessarily incorporate more than just the elements of English culture. Higginson asserted that "the English stock was transferred from an island to a continent, and mixed with new ingredients, that it might lose its quality of coarseness, and take on a more delicate grain" (228). The delicacy Higginson sought, in our literature, was somehow, he felt, compatible with "the American poet of passion . . . yet to come." He believed that the emotions of our poets were too "tame" and "manageable," that "there is no baptism of fire; no heat that breeds excess" (228)—in short, no Italy in the blood of our poets. Published first in 1870, this essay could not have been written in ignorance of Whitman, yet, as we shall see, Whitman was condemned because of his gross sensuality. The true poet of passion, for Higginson, would necessarily have the ardor of the Ideal. Even in fiction, he felt, there was scarcely a novel to suggest "that we modern Anglo-Saxons regard a profound human emotion as a thing worth painting." What he wanted was "hot blood . . . in the veins of literature" (230).

Of course there was France, and the French novel, as an enriching element for American culture. But the erstwhile minister felt that in French literature "the play of feeling is too naked and obvious"; in fact, "Puritan self-restraint is worth more than all that dissolute wealth" (230). The vestiges of Puritanism Higginson thought essential to American society and to an American literature. Not logically—but only historically—inconsistent with art, Puritanism was founded on a devotion to truth, he argued, as all art must be. And one liberating truth for modern American writing was the truth of the Ideal, addressed to the great American audience, a deep, popular heart, which would inspirit and arouse our best talents. "If we once lose faith in our audience," he concluded, "the muse grows silent" (235).

The character of the American audience constitutes a significant aspect of Higginson's critical premises. He believed that this popular heart was the repository of the moral and social values of the nation and that if the writer did not touch it deeply, he would lose his audience: "The public is right; it is the business of the writer, as of the speaker, to perfect the finer graces without sacrificing things more vital." He said that he thought that "a fine execution does not hinder acceptance in America, but rather aids it." But "where there is beauty of execution alone, a popular audience, even in America, very easily goes to sleep" (236). In touching on this relationship between values and art, Higginson took issue with proponents of art-for-art's-sake, for whom execution was virtually all. He had little sympathy for even Henry James, who had insisted that we must judge a writer on his treatment alone, not his subject. James was astute in recognizing that the deeper the artistic intelligence, the profounder the artist's moral vision. But Higginson preferred a more explicit affirmation of our national values. There is no doubt that the writer's writer often surrenders, in his devotion to the complexities of craft, the larger audience. And some *fin-de-siècle* artists who made a religion of art implied thereby a contempt for the public, which was alleged to be without taste. Yet the greatest artists have always created the taste by which they are enjoyed, and it goes without saying that a sophisticated taste and moral or democratic values are not incompatible.

Even so, Higginson recognized that the business of America, in the 1870s, was yet the creation of the nation. Ours was still a raw country, especially west of the Alleghenies, and there was not much refined social material in the interior of the nation. Henry James, among others, took the position that the thinness of our social order virtually prevented the development of a significant American literature. Writing in *Hawthorne* (1879), James argued that "it takes such an accumulation of history and custom, such a complexity of manners and types, to form a fund of suggestion for the novelist." And James enumerated the elements of "high civilization" which the American writer was forced to do without.

No State, in the European sense of the word, and indeed barely a specific national name. No sovereign, no court, no personal loyalty, no aristocracy, no church, no clergy, no army, no diplomatic service, no country gentlemen, no palaces, no castles, nor manors nor old country-houses, nor parsonages, nor thatched cottages nor ivied ruins; no cathedrals, nor abbeys, nor little Norman churches; no great Universities nor public schools—no Oxford nor Eton, nor Harrow; no literature, no novels, no museums, no pictures, no political society, no sporting class—no Epsom nor Ascot! Some such list as that might be drawn up of the absent things in American life. . . .[4]

Like Howells, Higginson was dismayed that James should have called Hawthorne provincial and should have designated as essential to the novelist those merely external "paraphernalia" of culture. The task of the American writer, Higginson felt, was to portray the drama of the social order in the act of defining itself. He thought "the play of human emotion" a thing "so absorbing" in itself that "the petty distinctions of cottage and castle become as nothing in its presence. Why not waive these small matters in advance, then, and go straight to the real thing?" The real thing would include the analysis of combinations of character that "only our national life produces," and the portrayal of "dramatic situations that belong to a clearer social atmosphere." Translated into art, these features would produce "the higher Americanism" (241) in literature. Higginson's ultimate faith in the potential of the American scene, for a high art, is expressed in his conclusion: "I affirm that democratic society, the society of the future, enriches and does not impoverish human life, and gives more, not less material for literary art" (239).

In his conclusion, then, Higginson echoed William Dean Howells, who observed of James's argument: "After leaving out all those novelistic 'properties,' as sovereigns, courts, aristocracy, gentry, castles, cottages, cathedrals, abbeys, universities, museums, political class, Epsoms, and Ascots, by the absence of which Mr. James suggests our poverty to the English conception, we have the whole of human life remaining, and a social structure presenting the only fresh and novel opportunities left to fiction, opportunities manifold and inexhaustible."[5] Yet James was never convinced by these two stalwart republicans. He told Howells that he believed that "it is on manners, customs, usages, habits, forms, upon all these things matured and established, that a novelist lives."[6] And the proof of his belief, he argued, was that America had not yet produced a novelist—a novelist, that is, in the class of Balzac or Thackeray. Against the claim that we had no Balzac or Thackeray, Howells and Higginson could not of course protest. But whether the cause of the matter was our lack of a sufficiently developed system of social institutions is a more complex issue which has been explored in greater detail in my study *The Novel of Manners in America*. Though we have had no Balzac or Thackeray, it is worth remarking that the social novels of James himself, as well as those of Howells, Edith Wharton, Sinclair Lewis, and others, go far toward refuting the alleged thinness of the American scene for a distinguished social art.[7]

In any event, Higginson's espousal of ideal values in the spiritual realm and democratic values in the social life of the nation endeared him to the larger public in his time—with the effect that he exercised a surprisingly great influence upon the national literary taste.

II *Criticism of Specific American Authors*

Aside from these general essays proclaiming Americanism in literature, Higginson's criticism is best exemplified in the biographies of Longfellow, Whittier, and Margaret Fuller—which I have already discussed—and in *Short Studies of American Authors* (1880), *Concerning All of Us* (1892), *The New World and the New Book* (1892), *Book and Heart: Essays on Literature and Life* (1897), *Contemporaries* (1899), *A Reader's History of American Literature* (1903), *Part of a Man's Life* (1905), and *Carlyle's Laugh, and Other*

Surprises (1909). Scattered critical observations are also given in other volumes like *Cheerful Yesterdays* (1898), but his major critical efforts appear in the works just named.

Obviously Higginson produced so much criticism of English, European, and American writers that no summary analysis could do it justice. Setting aside his remarks on English and Continental writers, as having had less impact on our literary history, we may nevertheless derive a just idea of his range and his insight by limiting our discussion to his criticism of individual American writers in three categories: (1) before the Concord era; (2) the Golden Age; and (3) the post-Civil War period. However brief, these notations of his critical positions will serve to suggest how he tried to solve "the equation of fame," which he called the first question of criticism.

III   *Before the Concord Era*

Higginson's major criticism of American writers before his time is contained in *A Reader's History of American Literature*. Addressed to the general reader and conventional in its overview of our literary production, this work was deeply indebted to Moses Coit Tyler's *A History of American Literature* (1879), which Higginson believed had rescued from oblivion" a "whole department of human history."[8] As he reviewed the Puritans, Higginson expressed admiration for Anne Bradstreet but averred that, like other Puritans, her taste in literature was "fatally compromised by religious prejudice," so that she turned away from the great Elizabethan models. Cotton Mather he thought too consciously artificial in style, while Edwards—whose theology Higginson abhorred—was "the highwater mark of Puritan prose." Franklin he regarded as "the first great writer of America," Irving as our first literary nationalist, while Cooper he surprisingly dismissed as a dull, artificial, "obnoxious, theoretical reformer."[9]

IV   *The Golden Age*

A Reader's History of American Literature is most instructive in its analysis of Higginson's youthful contemporaries. In fact, one reviewer observed that "to read the story of American literature from the hands of one who has taken part in the making of that literature and has known nearly all the men who have had most to do with giving it direction and position is very like the experience of the man immortalized by Browning who had seen and talked with Shelley."[10]

Emerson was of course "the controlling influence if not the creator of modern American thought."[11] Higginson had recognized the force of Emerson in his early youth, when he had told Harriet Prescott Spofford: "From Emerson, I differ . . . in temperament, attitude, and many conclusions; but in spite of this I know of no author whose writings seem to me so densely crowded with absolute truth, and so graceful in beauty"; although he admitted that there was "never any artistic wholeness in his Essays," they being "a series of exquisite sentences," yet "more than this I value . . . that noble calmness, gentleness, courage, and freedom; and that pure air and unflinching moral heroism which make him the very strongest teacher for the moral nature that this generation has given." He told her, "I know this by its fruits, in myself and my contemporaries."[12]

The essay "Ralph Waldo Emerson" properly introduces *Contemporaries*, since Emerson was the chief formative influence on Wentworth Higginson's mind. Emerson is credited with virtually the single-handed liberation of American literature from colonial bondage to England. Higginson's views should not surprise us, since the era before Emerson he believed to be singularly dry in imaginative effort, Fisher Ames having declared in "American Literature" (1807) that no literature could be possible under such conditions of social and economic equality. Cooper, Irving, and Bancroft had not yet appeared, and Sydney Smith seemed right, in 1818, when he observed that "there does not seem to be in America, at this moment, one man of considerable talents."[13]

Yet within two decades, according to Higginson, Emerson wrought a revolution in letters and liberated us from dependence on the "courtly Muses" of Europe. Higginson reviews Emerson's literary education at Harvard, under Edward Tyrrell Channing, and his early efforts in pedagogy and the ministry—all dedicated to the earnest and sincere instruction of his audience—and, in particular, to "killing the utility swine." His resignation from the pulpit, his marriages, his European travels, and his literary friends are all touched on as a preliminary to defining the significance of *Nature* (1836), *The Dial*, and "Thoughts on Modern Literature" as having—"in the comparative conventionalism of the literature of the period"—the effect of "a revelation" (10). Emerson is thus credited by Higginson with arousing "the first great need in the new literature—self-reliance." Through self-reliance, strong men and women were created; and "the first distinctly American movement in literature," Transcendental Romanticism, was born.

Higginson observed at the turn of the century that it was difficult to exaggerate the effect on the youth of the 1830s and 1840s of "Man Thinking," "Literary Ethics," *Nature*, and the "Divinity School Address," or "the extent to which their pithy and heroic maxims became a part of the very fibre of manhood to the generation then entering upon the stage of life" (14). Indeed, Higginson was one of those transformed youth. Emerson's subsequent publications are briefly cited, his international influence is sketched, his aphoristic genius is noted, his "exquisite melody touched with a certain wild grace" is praised, and his poetic use of the humble-bee and other American materials is absolved of the charge that it was "a foolish affectation of the familiar" (19).

Nevertheless, certain obvious difficulties trouble us in Higginson's review of Emerson's career. A great deal of valuable colonial and early Federalist literature is dismissed in claiming for Emerson the primacy he is granted. We may note that such an achievement as Emerson's must have had a long American foreground somewhere. We may or may not wish to ignore so readily the achievements of Anne Bradstreet, Cotton Mather, Jonathan Edwards, Benjamin Franklin, Philip Freneau, and Charles Brockden Brown. (Higginson could not, of course, have known Edward Taylor, who had not yet been discovered.)

Moreover, at the turn of the century, Emersonian Transcendentalism seemed antedeluvian—even to Higginson, as he prepared this volume. And certain obvious problems seem to have vexed him. The Civil War and the "all-absorbing interest of the new theories of evolution threw all the so-called transcendental philosophy into temporary shade" (15). (At least Higginson hoped that the shade was temporary.) He could not deny that Emerson's era had ended. Moreover, Emerson's limitations had become manifest; he could not compete with Darwin, Mill, Coleridge, Hegel, and Spencer as a systematic philosopher. Nor, obviously, from a review of his work, could he be called a coherent stylist. All Higginson could say was that Emerson was a philosopher only "in the vaguer ancient sense; his mission was to . . . offer profound and beautiful aphorisms, without even the vague thread of the Socratic method to tie them together" (16). Moreover, what could be said about a critic who called Hawthorne's *The Marble Faun* a "mere mush" and "discouraged young people from reading his books"; who had "a horror" of what he called "French correctness"; and who could rhyme *ground* with the ghastly *down'rd*? Higginson paid tribute to Emerson much as the later (mind-beclouded) Emerson had paid tribute to Longfellow: "that gentleman whose funeral we have been attending was a sweet and beautiful soul," Emerson had said, "but I forget his name" (22). So the post - Civil War era had forgotten Emerson's name. How could this have happened? Was the Concord Master not an immortal? Higginson hedged: "It must be left for future generations to determine Emerson's precise position . . ." (18).

In the case of "Amos Bronson Alcott" the issue was simpler. Alcott was something of a local spectacle—with his missionary experiment in socialistic pedagogy at Fruitlands and his doubtful "Concord Summer School of Philosophy"; his enigmatic "Orphic Sayings" in *The Dial* like "Love globes, Wisdom orbs everything"; and the otherworldly improvidence that reduced his family to penury. Emerson, Higginson suggests, made Alcott's reputation, but in the end he was a failure, even "in a manner 'an innocent charlatan' " (32). Nevertheless, Alcott was "among the most refined though not among the most powerful exponents of the ideal attitude" (24). Higginson had reason to remember appreciatively Alcott's "qualities of moral courage and physical courage which have in all ages been held essential to the true sage" (28). For on the night of the attempted rescue of the escaped slave Anthony Burns in 1854, when Higginson and others burst in the Court House door, Alcott had proved himself heroic. When the Court House steps had been cleared of protestors, Alcott had calmly climbed them, turned to the crowd, and said, "Why are we not inside?" When the mob seemed disinclined to follow him, he calmly descended the steps and went home. Although his theories were wildly impractical and every enigmatic utterance seemed "the worst shibboleth of that new bugbear, Transcendentalism" (27-28), Alcott redeemed himself for Higginson in that one sublime gesture.

An early admirer of Thoreau, and deeply influenced by his Transcendental nature essays, Higginson defended Thoreau from Lowell's "almost wanton misrepresentation" of the man in claiming that he was egotistical and antisocial. "The truth is," Higginson wrote, "Thoreau shared the noble protest against worldliness of what is called the 'transcendental' period in America, and naturally

shared some of the intellectual extravagances of that seething time;
but he did not, like some of his contemporaries, make his whims an
excuse for mere selfishness, and his home life—always the best
test—was thoroughly affectionate and faithful." He rejected the
view that Thoreau was "but a minor Emerson," claiming that he
had "the *lumen siccum*, or 'dry light,' . . . beyond all men of his
day." Thoreau's temperament he compared to "his native air in
winter,—clear, frosty, inexpressibly pure and bracing." He called
his imagination "daring," his power of literary appreciation
"something marvellous," and concluded that his poems on smoke,
mist, and haze "have an exquisite felicity of structure such as
nothing this side of the Greek anthology can equal."[14]

Higginson's criticism of Margaret Fuller, Longfellow, and Whittier I have already touched on, in the section on his biographies.
But something deserves to be said about his criticism of Lowell and
Holmes. Higginson was a childhood friend of Jimmy Lowell and
always admired the poet, though considerable ambivalence confuses his estimate of the artist. Vexed by Lowell's less than radical
position on abolition, Higginson in 1891 could still call Lowell's
"Commemoration Ode" "the finest single poem yet produced in
this country"[15] and observe, improbably, that "no American author,
unless it be Emerson, has achieved a securer hold upon a lasting
fame."[16] A few years later, however, in *Old Cambridge* (1899), he
remarked that Lowell "never quite attained to smoothness or finish
in utterance," was "always liable to be entangled by his own wealth
of thought," and was "constantly led . . . into confused rhetoric
and mixed metaphors."[17] Holmes, on the other hand, produced
bland verse "of uniform smoothness and elegance; and as the best
of them are marked by fineness rather than depth of feeling, it is
not likely that a freer treatment would have increased their
power."[18]

Higginson was generous in praising Poe's greater inventive gifts,
asserting that his place in purely imaginative prose-writing is "as
unquestionable as Hawthorne's." But he criticized Poe's lack of
spiritual depth, the "low moral tone" of his criticism, and the ex-
cesses of his private life, which Griswold had done so much to sen-
sationalize, with the effect that he could only conclude: "After all,
the austere virtues—the virtues of Emerson and Whittier—afford
the best soil for genius."[19]

None of these writers, in any event, equaled Hawthorne in
Higginson's personal "equation of fame." The first artist "to see

that we truly have, for romantic purposes, a past; two hundred years being really quite enough to constitute antiquity," Hawthorne, for Higginson, was the perfect blend of historical awareness, spiritual idealism, and profound symbolic understanding. In full possession of his gifts from the first, and always in marvelous command of his art, Hawthorne was "a source of more tonic influence for young writers, through all coming time."[20]

V   The Post - Civil War Period

As the age of Emerson and Whittier passed, giving way to the local-color writers of the South and West and to the new Realists and the younger Naturalists, Higginson's spiritual idealism became a less pertinent platform from which to issue critical pronouncements. A writer like Sidney Lanier he could of course praise, for Lanier's poems were "daring, impetuous, bristling with strophe and anti-strophe, with dramatic appeal and response, but always single-minded, noble, and pure. . . ."[21] But what could be said about Walt Whitman?

"The rhythmic apostle of democracy," Whitman was always a vexing problem for Higginson. Higginson implies that Whitman's fame was created by the British, who were first to appreciate the "personal picturesqueness" of an odd American type comparable to Artemus Ward and Josh Billings. Higginson noted that "much of the vague sentiment of democracy in his works, while wholly picturesque and novel to an Englishman,—provided that he can tolerate it at all,—is to us comparatively trite and almost conventional." The expurgated British editions, moreover, omitted "all the malodorous portions of Whitman's earlier poems," and the rest was a Fourth of July oration "in what is not even plain verse."[22]

Higginson had difficulty in justifying Emerson's initial praise of *Leaves of Grass*, but he took some satisfaction in Emerson's distaste for Whitman's "priapism" in *Calamus* and *The Children of Adam*. Nor could Higginson quite accommodate himself to E. C. Stedman's placing Whitman "among the *Dei majores* of our literature" in *Poets of America*, explaining it as an act of friendship in a critic whose taste had slipped.

For Higginson, Whitman was a latter-day Ossian, a Martin Tupper of his times, whose "mere revolt against the tyranny of form" would not secure immortality "to the author of the experiment" (77). He had little respect for Whitman's catalogue devices, his use of epanaphora, "his sandy wastes of iteration" (84), or his neologisms. A dandy in verse, Whitman never reached "the honest consciousness of the classes he most celebrates,—the drover, the teamster, the soldier" (83), and, lacking that "personal and ideal side of passion which alone can elevate and dignify it," the "grossness of the sensual side of his poems" (80) was therefore accentuated. Higginson conceded to Whitman some of the "highest ingredients" of a poet's imagination—"a keen eye, a ready sympathy, a strong touch, a vivid but not shaping imagination" (84). But the very inspiration that aroused Whitman implied for Higginson a weakness "on the personal side leading to pruriency and on the rational side to rant" (79).

These literary views suggest the myopia—and the insight—that often characterize a contemporary estimate. We may be much more sympathetic to Whitman's organic theory of verse, to the revolutionary embodiment of the Self in *Leaves of Grass*, and to his democratic sympathies than Higginson was, and yet concede that Whitman could rant, become tedious and discomfit through failures of literary taste. Yet in *Leaves of Grass* Whitman created a sublime work of the American imagination, flawed certainly, but without parallel in the nineteenth century. Higginson's rigid respect for formalism in poetry and his genteel moralism—not unexpected in a Christian minister turned critic—led him to reverence too much the spiritually uplifting Ideal, against which all verse and conduct were to be tested. Viewed from this perspective, Whitman fell below the moral mark. Add to this Higginson's indignation at the legends of Whitman's service to soldiers in the Civil War—when the colonel and others had taken the Rebel fire—and the sources of his distaste for Whitman are clear—clear but not compelling.

Higginson's criticism of the local-color tradition was characteristically ambivalent. Steeped in the literature of New England, he could not of course logically object to the prose of other regionalists. He took satisfaction that "the labors of many authors, in all parts of our vast country, are gradually putting on record a wide range of local types." Yet what he admired and disliked in these types is interesting. He found in Sarah Orne Jewett's fiction an "element of higher breeding and more refined living," her people "more influenced by sentiment, perhaps sometimes too much so"; while Mary Wilkins Freeman's people were "wonders of keen delineation"—their lives, however, "sometimes too grim." As a rule, he observed, "it is the less educated classes which are more easily drawn, though not necessarily or always the most worth drawing."[23] Few local colorists seemed able to portray a lady or a gentleman, with the effect that Bret Harte was merely picturesque, Joaquin Miller all cowboy boots and buckskin fringes, and Garland effective but somber.

Mark Twain, Higginson felt, was "one of the really great jesters of the world," but Higginson apparently saw little in Twain beyond the comic buffoon. *Adventures of Huckleberry Finn*—while marking "a distinct step forward in American literature"[24]—did not suggest to Higginson that deeper probing of American racial relations which others have commended.

Though masterly at the depiction of ladies and gentlemen, Henry James shows up another blind spot in Higginson's critical vision. The colonel found James's characters thin and lacking in manliness, his early prose style hurried, and his criticism prolix and lacking in "symmetry of structure and steadiness of hand."[25] Higginson deplored James's satire on the New England character in *The Europeans* and suffragist reform in *The Bostonians*. James's failures as a writer Higginson traced to his lack of training in the classics and the absence of an invigorating contact with "the mass of mankind." But the chief source of his criticism was James's feeling about the thinness of America as a social setting and the impoverishment of its materials for the artist. "When he says, for instance, that a monarchical society is 'more available for the novelist than any other,' he shows," Higginson argued, "that he does not quite appreciate the strong point of republicanism, in that it develops real individuality in proportion as it diminishes conventional distinctions. The truth is," he observed, "that the modern novel has risen with the advance of democratic society, on the ruins of feudalism."[26] Yet years later, when he came to write the *Reader's History of American Literature*, Higginson could not help observing that "there are no stories in modern literature quite as good as James's best." Singling out "Madame de Mauves" and "The Madonna of the Future" for praise, Higginson acknowledged that few authors had "ever touched with more delicate precision the vexed question of morality in art."[27]

Howells, on the other hand, was generally more admirable, for he had not only "delicacy of handling" and fineness and firmness of touch" but also "that local coloring to which Mr. James is so provokingly indifferent."[28] Higginson praised Howells for "really contributing important studies to the future organization of our society. How is it to be stratified? How much weight is to be given to intellect, to character, to wealth, to antecedents, to inheritance? Not only must a republican nation meet and solve these problems," he observed, "but the solution is more assisted by the writers of romances than by the compilers of statistics."[29] Higginson thought that the early novels of Howells were rather insubstantial but that with *Silas Lapham, Annie Kilburn,* and *A Hazard of New Fortunes* (which had been influenced by the social morality and aesthetic of Tolstoy and Turgenev), Howells had achieved great distinction in celebrating the dignity and native worth of the individual American, which Higginson thought to be the basis of any democratic art. Although the mode of Realism in fiction was moderately distasteful to him, because it subordinated ideality to actuality, what might be to what is, Higginson nevertheless conceded the triumph of Howells and his school, though feeling always that the pendulum of taste would swing back again toward the purer spirituality of Hawthorne's best work.

Higginson's genteel critical views may suggest that he had little appreciation for the young Naturalists in the 1890s and thereafter. Such an impression would be partly mistaken. Although he deplored Norris as a "worshipper of Zola,"[30] even while admiring Norris's Western settings, the colonel was full of high praise for Crane's *The Red Badge of Courage* when it appeared in 1895. Although many Union veterans had denounced the book as unpatriotic, Higginson remarked "the extraordinary freshness and vigor of the book." He noted "the breathlessness, the hurry, the confusion, the seeming aimlessness, as of a whole family of disturbed ants, running to and fro, yet somehow accomplishing something at last; all these aspects, which might seem the most elementary and the easiest to depict, are yet those surest to be omitted, not merely by the novelists, but by the regimental histories themselves." Comparing Crane to Tolstoy, he praised Crane's decision to tell the story from the point of view of a pawn in the action. "The wonder is that this young writer, who had no way of getting at the facts except through the gossip—printed or written—of these very old soldiers, should be able to go behind them all, and give an account of their life, not only more vivid than they themselves have ever given, but more accurate." Calling the novel "A Bit of War Photography," he concluded that it had "that marvellous intuitive quality which for want of a better name we call genius."[31] In a comparable identification of young genius, Higginson, at eighty-two, called attention to Edith Wharton, claiming that her new book *The House of Mirth* (1905) seemed to him "to stand at the head of all American fiction, save Hawthorne alone."[32]

VI *Emily Dickinson: The Shock of Recognition*

While all of these observations have their interest in revealing Higginson as a critic compelling himself to stay abreast of his times, probably his greatest service to American letters was his fortuitous "discovery" of Emily Dickinson and his uneasy encouragement of her poetic genius. She had doubtless known of his liberal Christian ministry in Worcester, his antislavery agitation, and his graceful nature essays. But it was his "Letter to a Young Contributor" that provoked her to reach out to him in early 1862.

In this *Atlantic* article of advice to would-be writers, Higginson had remarked that young writers ought really to digest and assimilate their experience before attempting to express it. The literary art was a severe discipline, he warned. "Oftentimes a word shall speak what accumulated volumes have labored in vain to utter; there may be years of crowded passion in a word, and half a life in a sentence. Such being the majesty of the art you seek to practice," he told his novices, "you can at least take time and deliberation before dishonoring it." He urged young writers to charge their style with life, aim at clarity, "demonstrate to others the merit of your own performance. If your work does not vindicate itself, you cannot vindicate it." In what must have been a telling phrase for Emily Dickinson, he wrote: "Have faith enough in your own individuality to keep it down for a year or so." And "remember how many great writers have created the taste by which they were enjoyed, and do not be in a hurry." Still, he observed, "do not be made conceited by obscurity any more than by notoriety. Many fine geniuses have been long neglected. . . ."[33]

Emily Dickinson was clearly intrigued by Higginson's discussion of the intensity of the buried life, the discipline of literary art, and the possible necessity of deferring publication until the apprenticeship had been served. In April 1862 she wrote to him an enigmatic letter, each sentence a paragraph: "Mr. Higginson, Are you too deeply occupied to say if my verse is alive? The mind is so near itself it cannot see distinctly, and I have none to ask. Should you think it breathed, and had you the leisure to tell me, I should feel quick gratitude. If I make the mistake, that you dared to tell me would give me sincerer honor toward you. I inclose my name, asking you, if you please, sir, to tell me what is true? That you will not betray me it is needless to ask, since honor is its own pawn."[34]

Her letter, in its stylistic oddity, was beguiling enough. But Higginson experienced the shock of recognition when he read the four brief poems she had enclosed with her letter—"Safe in their alabaster chambers," "I'll tell you how the sun rose," "We play at paste," and "The nearest dream recedes unrealized." The colonel had "the impression of a wholly new and original poetic genius," but he was baffled by the complexities of her perception and utterance and vexed by the eccentricity of her unorthodox poetic form.

He replied, thanking her for her poems, and expressing a criticism, now lost, which she took as "surgery." In her reply she evaded a number of personal questions he had posed and even misrepresented the number of verses she had composed, saying, "I made no verse, but one or two, until this winter, sir,"[35] when in fact she had already written several hundred poems. Included with her reply were other poems manifesting what Higginson came to call "that defiance of form, never through carelessness, and never precisely from whim."[36] By June he had told her that her verses "jingled" and that she perhaps ought to delay publication until she had more fully mastered the formal aspects of conventional poetry. Publication, she countered, was foreign to her; that, if it were her destiny, fame would come of itself; and that her "barefoot rank" was better. Nevertheless, she asked him to be her friend and literary "preceptor."

Emily Dickinson, it must be said, was but one of scores of women, young and old, who had sent their manuscripts to Higginson for criticism and encouragement. In view of the flood of mail his *Atlantic* essays invariably provoked and the chore of replying, and in view of his imminent departure for South Carolina, to assume command of the First South Carolina Volunteers, it is remarkable that Higginson even noticed Emily Dickinson. Nevertheless, to his credit, he did, and for nearly a quarter of a century they corresponded, at varying intervals, until her death in 1886.

Their correspondence is uniformly marked by her steady affectation of the role of a pupil, and, on his part, by an acceptance of "a preceptorship which it is almost needless to say did not exist."[37] After eight years of her coy epistolary exchanges, he went down to

Amherst to meet her. His account of their meeting is too long to
quote here, though it is a remarkable document of reminiscence
about an elusive, still little understood poet. Suffice it to say that
she struck him as nunlike, peculiar, and enigmatic, compulsive in
her talk, which he found disconnected and miscellaneous. "She was
much too enigmatical a being for me to solve in an hour's inter-
view," he later wrote, "and an instinct told me that the slightest
attempt at direct cross-examination would make her withdraw into
her shell; I could only sit still and watch, as one does in the woods; I
must name my bird without a gun, as recommended by Emerson."[38] He saw her only one other time, briefly.

In view of his criticism of her formal unorthodoxy and his advice
that she delay publication, Higginson has sometimes been made out
to be a villain of genteel-era criticism who repressed a profoundly
great poetic genius reaching out to him for encouragement. Thomas
H. Johnson is representative of Dickinson admirers who have made
Higginson's discouragement the chief cause of her failure to publish
in her lifetime. Is the charge justified?

There is no doubt that Emily Dickinson eluded Higginson's grasp
in the 1860s. Her mind was too swift, mercurial, too inspired with
paradox and metaphor, to be wholly understood by the kindly and
well-meaning colonel. Even later, in the 1890s, when he had
restudied the hundred or so poems she had mailed to him, he still
expressed bafflement with her genius. (Modesty may lead many
readers of her poetry to confess a similar baffled respect!)
Nevertheless, Higginson was conscious that she was a wholly
original poetic mind. If she did not care to publish, we ought to
recognize that there were more complex reasons than his initial discouragement. She regarded publication, it is worth remembering, as
"the auction of the mind," and she became morbidly intent on her
poetic privacy, and even personally withdrew altogether from the
world. What her compulsive and disconnected talk, enigmatic
letters, her poetic themes, aversion from publication, and deepen-
ing seclusion may reflect is a serious emotional disturbance in a
woman of brilliant gifts. It subtracts nothing from her literary
genius to acknowledge that her verse was extremely difficult to
most of the people who knew of it. And to those—like Higginson
and Helen Hunt Jackson—who recognized her gifts, she turned
away when the subject was publication. Helen Hunt Jackson wrote
to her: "I have a little manuscript volume with a few of your verses
in it—and I read them very often. You are a great poet—and it is a

wrong to the day you live in, that you will not sing aloud. When you are what men call dead, you will be sorry you were so stingy."[39] Nevertheless, to such appeals Emily Dickinson closed the valves of her attention, like stone.

Whether or not Higginson's discouragement was the principal reason for her refusal to publish in her lifetime—which seems doubtful—there is no question that he was instrumental in making her poems available after her death. For when Mabel Loomis Todd, a friend of the Dickinsons, approached him in 1889 with a plan for editing some of the manuscript poems found after her death, Higginson was intrigued by the project. He had some doubts about the public's willingness to accept the work of so irregular a poet, but on reading the poems in Mrs. Todd's possession, he wrote: "I can't tell you how much I am enjoying these poems. There are many new to me which take my breath away & which also have *form* beyond most of those I have seen before. . . . My confidence in their *availability* is greatly increased."[40] One may hope that these new poems sent him back to those that Emily Dickinson had first mailed to him, in the 1860s, for they are among her best. In any event, *Poems of Emily Dickinson*, coedited with Mrs. Todd, appeared in 1890.

It is as Emily Dickinson's editor that Higginson performed a signal service for American letters but, at the same time, failed in a serious editorial responsibility. His failure lay in his taking the liberty of affixing titles to her verses, of rearranging stanzas, and of "correcting" oddities of her grammar and usage. Such "creative editing" (as that common practice might have been termed in the nineteenth century) is wholly anathema today; no editor has the right to tamper with or corrupt an author's text by imposing on it his presumed "improvements." But the practice was less reprehensible then, and may have seemed justified by the confused state of her manuscripts—many poems existing in several different forms, with no indication as to which was the final or intended version. Nevertheless, though it is to Higginson's everlasting discredit that he altered the poems in ways we now condemn, he yet deserves approbation for exerting himself so fully in her behalf after her death. When the 1890 volume appeared, he wrote to Mrs. Todd: "Books just arrived—bound. I am *astounded* in looking through. How could we have doubted them?" And when the first series sold well and Mrs. Todd broached the idea of another volume, *Poems of Emily Dickinson: Second Series* (1891), the colonel told her: "Let us alter as little as possible now that the public ear is opened."[41]

Although Higginson did not fully understand or appreciate the extraordinary gift of Emily Dickinson during her lifetime, and although he was dismayed by her irregularity, doubting the capacity of the public to respond to her art, he had perhaps a livelier appreciation than any of his contemporaries, once she was published, of the special qualities of this extraordinary poet. Though he erred in "improving" her verses, it was through his direct agency that her work was first made available to the public. In partial defense of Higginson, it should perhaps be remarked that, even after the publication of her poetry, her talent was not everywhere appreciated. Few in England immediately admired her, and the second series of poems was rejected by British publishers. Emily Dickinson's reputation as one of the great American poets is a twentieth-century phenomenon.

CHAPTER 9

Epilogue: Higginson and the Equation of Fame

AS a writer Higginson is perhaps most memorable for his brief sketches of important contemporaries like Emerson, Thoreau, Lowell, Margaret Fuller, Wendell Phillips, Garrison, Bronson Alcott, Holmes, and Whittier. Taken singly, these charming personal reminiscences may seem negligible. But taken together, they create a vivid picture of the Concord-Cambridge milieu in the great age of the Transcendental Newness and the revolutionary abolition movement. Shaped by the major literary and political currents of his time, Higginson made his portraits come to life for us as almost no other writer of the time was able to do. Though Higginson lacked a deep analytic mind, Howard W. Hintz has rightly remarked that "with his natural love of people, his wide capacity for rich and varied friendships, his propensity for anecdote, and his remarkably retentive memory, he was to the manner born in the realm of intimate biography, reminiscence, and autobiography."[1] Something of a Boswellian figure reflected in the glory of his subjects, Higginson outlived them all, and achieved a lesser greatness thanks to the lucidity and charm of a richly varied style that made him extraordinarily popular throughout the country.

Higginson's moral fervor and adherence to the "rules" has inevitably led him to be grouped with Thomas Bailey Aldrich, E. C. Stedman, and Hamilton Wright Mabie as an exemplar of the Genteel Tradition in criticism. To a great extent this classification is accurate, for Higginson always affirmed good taste—the taste of ladies and gentlemen—in the writer's choice of subject and in his execution. He held high standards of style, based on the classics, and deplored wayward genius defiant of form. Yet his fiery abolitionism, his radical views on social democracy, and his labor in

148

behalf of woman's suffrage—together with his sometimes perplexed appreciation of writers as diverse as Dickinson, Crane, Howells, and Wharton—suggest that it would be a serious mistake to identify him too closely with those genteel-era contemporaries.

As a poet, Higginson's talent was negligible, though his Romantic verses reveal a competent craftsman skilled enough in mere technique, but lacking a creative imagination. Nevertheless, he rendered a useful service to the poetic criticism of his time in exploring—intelligently, on the whole—the merits of Emerson and Thoreau, Holmes and Lowell, and Helen Hunt Jackson and Sidney Lanier. His moral and aesthetic biases blinded him to some of the unorthodox achievements of Poe, Whitman, and Dickinson. Yet he was candid enough to acknowledge, uneasily, the force of their poetry. As a novelist and sporadic short-story writer, Higginson was comparably limited—*Malbone, The Monarch of Dreams,* and other tales being clearly works of a minor order. His models—Hawthorne and Austen—were suitable, but they failed to unify in his imagination, so that he excelled neither as a novelist nor as a romancer. Of the fiction he produced, only *The Monarch of Dreams* still interests—largely, though, as a revelation of deep unconscious impulses fascinatingly deployed as dream symbols of inner conflict. Recognizing the thinness of his narrative achievement, he wisely abandoned fiction.

At his best, Higginson's essays on Nature approach Thoreau's in appreciation, though not in intellectual power, and lead directly to the work of John Muir and John Burroughs. While nature studies like his "Water Lilies," "The Life of Birds," "Snow," and "April Days" do not yield much in the way of knowledge, they reveal an attentive witness to the ways of the winds and tides, the bluejays and butterflies, the thistles and wood-anemones. Celebrations of the natural order, these essays richly record Higginson's sense of the "lessons of faith and beauty"[2] communicated by external nature, the veil of the noumenal Spirit, or what Goethe had called "the living garment of God." So winsome are his meditations on the flora and fauna of the Cambridge and Newport environs that Hintz has even called his nature studies "comparable with the best American writing that has been done in this form." And Fred L. Pattee, in *History of American Literature Since 1870,* has praised him for avoiding "the over-literary element on the one hand and the over-scientific on the other," with the effect that he became "the first of what may be called the modern school of nature writers."[3]

As a biographer and historian, Higginson excelled only in occasional moments, chiefly when dealing with artists whom he had personally known or with events in which he had directly participated. None of the biographies is definitive—although the studies of Longfellow and Margaret Fuller stood up for a number of years. Superseded now in every way, they are still works of sustained (though superficial) narrative portraiture, enlivened by personal reminiscence and anecdote. The less than original scholarship they reveal also characterizes his historical prose, which was useful in its own time but has also been totally superseded. As Romantic history, done better by Bancroft and Parkman, Higginson's historical prose yet made up a tributary in the mighty stream of patriotic chronicle that shaped the nineteenth-century sense of America's "manifest destiny." Lucidly written, lively, and informative, they served especially well the young people of their day, but have not survived in that great tribunal to which he always appealed—the public mind. Similarly, his social criticism—diversified and finally superficial—remains interesting only for the student of American radical thought. Most effective when the issues were apparently black and white, when an Absolute Principle could be invoked, his argumentative prose has faded with the causes later won. Yet his account of the attempted rescue of the slave Anthony Burns, of his ride through Kansas during the border wars, of his command of black troops during the Civil War, and of his feminist and temperance campaigns are told in a stirring prose charged with high moral fervor. Later, after the Civil War, he was, like most observers, baffled by the complexities of our newly developing industrial order, by economic issues like free trade and imperialism. Yet he always retained a genuine liberal spirit, and espoused social democracy and a respect for the people, as against the oligarchies of entrenched wealth and power.

We must finally rank Wentworth Higginson as a writer and critic of the second order. But as an individual, as a man of his time, he was remarkable. A man of high moral principle, a gentleman, a man without meanness or rancor, high-minded, devoted to literature and culture in the Arnoldian sense of the best that had been thought and said, a defender of human dignity and of the respect due the individual—whatever his or her race, creed, sex, politics, or national origin—committed to action in behalf of social democracy, preeminently a man of character and personal integrity, of deep compassion and wide sympathies—Wentworth Higginson is a memorable example of what an American man of letters in the nineteenth century could be.

For the reader who is drawn to him, there is no more revealing introduction to the man and writer than his attractive autobiography *Cheerful Yesterdays* (1898). Composed in his seventies, this retrospective of his whole life from the early Cambridge days forward is admirably free of the egotism common in autobiographies. For although Higginson was a man of great prominence in his time, he had the humility to acknowledge "his own extreme unimportance."[4] He was moved to record his times and his own life, but only for whatever benefit they might have to posterity: "When I think of the vast changes which every man of my time has seen, and of the men and women whom I have known,—those who created American literature and who freed millions of slaves,—men and women whom, as the worldly-wise Lord Houghton once wrote me, 'Europe has learned to honour, and would do well to imitate,' then I feel, that whether I will or no, something worth chronicling may be included in the proposed chapters."[5]

Cheerful Yesterdays preserves a fine balance between Higginson's private life and the public history of his time from the 1840s through the 1890s. His account of the Transcendental period, the abolitionist movement, the Civil War, and the literary life of the 1870s cannot of course be taken in isolation from other accounts of these events, for a necessary element of impressionism pervades the work. Nevertheless, in terms of what he observed, his responses are generally faithful to the actualities of his time. Moreover, as a record of his private life, *Cheerful Yesterdays* is informed with that sweetness of temper and undefinable charisma that made him always attractive to his contemporaries. And it is a rich treasury of interpretive personal history, reminiscence, and anecdote. Howard Mumford Jones has even called it a "masterpiece," remarking that "such is the conventional-mindedness of literary historians, they do not recognize the autobiography as an art form. Nevertheless, American letters have produced a great number of these admirable memoirs, and the long golden afternoon of New England gave us a whole library of them, of which Higginson's is one of the most charming."[6]

As he ended the work, Higginson felt that many of the "most important" spiritual events of his life had gone unrecorded. Nevertheless, though his career belonged to his own time, he rightly believed that the record of it would be "chiefly valuable for the light it throws on the period and the place."[7] As a reformer, he lived long enough to see many of his ideals realized in the social transformation of the nation. Nevertheless, he felt that much yet remained to be done, and he expressed the wish, toward the close of his life, that he would "live to see international arbitration secured, civil service reform completed, free trade established; to find the legal and educational rights of the two sexes equalized; to know that all cities are as honestly governed as that in which I dwell; to see natural monopolies owned by the public, not in private hands; to see drunkenness extirpated; to live under absolute as well as nominal religious freedom; to perceive American literature to be thoroughly emancipated from the habit of colonial deference which still hampers it." He hoped, and indeed believed it possible, that "after the progress already made on the whole in these several directions, some future generation may see the fulfillment of what remains." His final words—they constitute the motto of his life—were those of the French iconoclast Proudhon: "Let my memory perish, if only humanity may be free."[8]

Notes and References

Preface

1. Henry James, review of Thomas Wentworth Higginson's *Cheerful Yesterdays* in *Literature* (London), June 11, 1898; quoted in Anna Mary Wells, *Dear Preceptor: The Life and Times of Thomas Wentworth Higginson* (Boston, 1963), p. 316.

Chapter One

1. Mary Thacher Higginson, *Thomas Wentworth Higginson: The Story of His Life* (Boston, 1914; reprinted New York, 1971), pp. 15 - 16.
2. Ibid., p. 7.
3. Thomas Wentworth Higginson, *Cheerful Yesterdays* (Boston, 1898; reprinted New York, 1968), p. 20.
4. Ibid., p. 38.
5. Mary T. Higginson, pp. 16 - 17.
6. Among Edward Tyrell Channing's students were Ralph Waldo Emerson, Henry David Thoreau, Oliver Wendell Holmes, Charles Francis Adams, Charles Sumner, Edward Everett Hale, James Lothrop Motley, Charles Eliot Norton, and James Russell Lowell. Cf. Wells, *Dear Preceptor*, p. 21.
7. Mary T. Higginson, p. 25.
8. Ibid., pp. 29 - 30.
9. Ibid., p. 30.
10. Thomas Wentworth Higginson, *Contemporaries* (Boston, 1899), p. 10.
11. Ralph Waldo Emerson, "Historic Notes on Life and Letters in New England," in *The American Transcendentalists*, ed. Perry Miller (Garden City, N.Y., 1957), p. 5.
12. William Ellery Channing, "A Participant's Definition," in *The American Transcendentalists*, p. 36.
13. Ibid., p. 37.
14. Ibid., p. 38.
15. Perry Miller, "Foreword," *The American Transcendentalists*, p. [ix].
16. T. W. Higginson, *Cheerful Yesterdays*, pp. 35 - 36.
17. Ibid., pp. 77 - 78.
18. Mary T. Higginson, pp. 60 - 61.

19. Ibid., p. 45.
20. Ibid., p. 44.
21. Ibid., p. 64.
22. Ibid., pp. 52 - 53.
23. Ibid., pp. 31 - 32.
24. Ibid., pp. 34, 43, 47.
25. Ibid., pp. 51 - 52.
26. T. W. Higginson, *Cheerful Yesterdays*, p. 92.
27. Mary T. Higginson, p. 58.
28. Octavius B. Frothingham, *Transcendentalism in New England: A History* (New York, 1876; reprinted New York, 1959), p. 153.
29. Mary T. Higginson, p. 63.
30. Ibid., p. 49.
31. Ibid., pp. 64 - 65.
32. Ibid., pp. 63 - 64.
33. Ibid., p. 46.
34. T. W. Higginson, *Cheerful Yesterdays*, p. 98.
35. Ibid., p. 101.
36. Quoted in Tilden G. Edelstein, *Strange Enthusiasm: A Life of Thomas Wentworth Higginson* (New Haven, 1968), p. 54.
37. Ibid., p. 56.
38. Mary T. Higginson, p. 71.
39. Ibid., p. 74.
40. Ibid., p. 76.
41. Ibid., pp. 78 - 79.
42. Ibid., p. 42.
43. Ibid., pp. 80, 82.
44. Quoted in Edelstein, p. 65.
45. Ibid., pp. 66 - 67.
46. Edelstein, p. 76.
47. Mary T. Higginson, p. 87.
48. Edelstein, p. 77.
49. Mary T. Higginson, p. 91.
50. Ibid., p. 92.
51. Howard N. Meyer, *Colonel of the Black Regiment: The Life of Thomas Wentworth Higginson* (New York, 1967), p. 52.
52. Mary T. Higginson, p. 73.
53. T. W. Higginson, *Cheerful Yesterdays*, pp. 120 - 21.
54. Mary T. Higginson, pp. 95 - 96.
55. T. W. Higginson, *Cheerful Yesterdays*, p. 119.
56. Mary T. Higginson, p. 103.
57. Ibid., p. 89.
58. Quoted in Edelstein, p. 88.
59. *Letters and Journals of Thomas Wentworth Higginson, 1846 - 1906*, ed. Mary Thacher Higginson (New York, 1969), p. 19.

60. Mary T. Higginson, p. 105.
61. Ibid., p. 104.
62. Ibid.
63. Ibid., p. 110.
64. T. W. Higginson, *Cheerful Yesterdays,* pp. 122 - 23.
65. Mary T. Higginson, p. 97.
66. Ibid., p. 96.
67. Ibid., p. 88.
68. *Letters and Journals . . .,* p. 15.
69. Mary T. Higginson, p. 88.
70. Ibid., p. 98.
71. *Letters and Journals . . .,* p. 23.
72. Henry David Thoreau, *Walden and Civil Disobedience* (New York, 1966), p. 232.
73. Quoted in Edelstein, p. 102.
74. Ibid.
75. Ibid., p. 105.
76. Ibid., pp. 105 - 106.
77. Ibid., p. 115.
78. Mary T. Higginson, p. 112.
79. T. W. Higginson, *Cheerful Yesterdays,* pp. 130 - 31.
80. Wells, pp. 83 - 84.
81. Quoted in Edelstein, p. 152.
82. Mary T. Higginson, p. 144.
83. Ibid., p. 145.
84. Ibid.
85. Quoted in Edelstein, p. 159.
86. Ibid., p. 118.
87. Ibid., p. 162.
88. T. W. Higginson, *Cheerful Yesterdays,* p. 166.
89. Mary T. Higginson, p. 173.
90. Ibid., pp. 178 - 79.
91. Ibid., p. 190.
92. Quoted in Edelstein, p. 233.
93. Ibid., p. 199.
94. Mary T. Higginson, p. 210.
95. Meyer, p. 244.
96. To Mrs. Howe, Higginson later wrote: "Our Oldport will always be dear. The new-Newport . . . seems a sort of dusty daylight place that must be hard to dream in; in which picturesque, romantic, unique figures . . . have no part. *Letters and Journals . . .,* p. 232.
97. Quoted in Edelstein, p. 304.
98. Ibid., pp. 302, 304.
99. "The Next Great Question," *Independent,* November 12, 1868; quoted in Edelstein, p. 318.

100. Mary T. Higginson, pp. 296 - 97.

101. Quoted in Edelstein, p. 297.

102. Mary T. Higginson, p. 263.

103. "Introduction," *The Works of Epictetus* (Boston, 1866), p. ix.

104. Mary T. Higginson, p. 262.

105. Howard Mumford Jones, "Introduction," *Army Life in a Black Regiment* (East Lansing, Michigan, 1960), p. ix.

106. Mary T. Higginson, p. 282.

107. Ibid., p. 278.

108. Ibid., p. 280.

109. Ibid., p. 284.

110. Howard W. Hintz, *Thomas Wentworth Higginson: Disciple of the Newness* (New York, 1939), pp. 2 - 3.

111. Mary T. Higginson, p. 265.

112. William Dean Howells, *A Chance Acquaintance* (Boston, 1874), p. 9.

113. Mary T. Higginson, p. 276.

114. Ibid., pp. 286 - 87.

115. Ibid., p. 290.

116. Ibid., pp. 294 - 95.

117. Ibid., p. 304; Edelstein, p. 399.

118. "The Worcester Convention," *Woman's Journal*, November 6, 1880; quoted in Edelstein, p. 368.

119. Edelstein, pp. 369, 372.

120. Ibid., p. 378.

121. "Step by Step," *Nationalist*, 1 (1889), p. 147.

122. Edelstein, pp. 382 - 83.

123. Ibid., p. 385.

124. "Where Liberty Is Not, There Is My Country," *Harper's Bazar*, 32 (1899), p. 671.

125. Boston *Evening Transcript*, May 10, 1899; quoted in Edelstein, p. 389.

126. Quoted in Edelstein, p. 390.

127. Ibid., p. 391.

128. Boston *Evening Transcript*, June 1, 1909; quoted in Edelstein, p. 392.

Chapter Two

1. *T. W. Higginson*, "The Sympathy of Religions," *Studies in History and Letters* (Boston, 1900), p. 318. Citations from this work will hereafter be noted in parentheses in the text.

2. Quoted in Mary T. Higginson, p. 268.

3. *Letters and Journals* . . ., p. 350.

4. Meyer, p. 108.

5. Quoted in Edelstein, p. 317.

6. Quoted in Meyer, p. 112.

7. T. W. Higginson, "Saints and Their Bodies," in *Outdoor Papers* (Boston, 1886), p. 5.

8. T. W. Higginson, "Introduction," *The Works of Epictetus*, pp. iii, ix - x.

9. H. M. Jones, "Introduction," *Army Life in a Black Regiment*, pp. vii - ix.

10. Quoted in Mary T. Higginson, p. 270.

11. Jones, p. ix.

Chapter Three

1. Ralph Waldo Emerson, "Fate," *Selections from Ralph Waldo Emerson*, ed. Stephen E. Whicher (Boston, 1957), p. 308.

2. Mary T. Higginson, p. 68.

3. T. W. Higginson, *Army Life in a Black Regiment* (Boston, 1900), pp. 4 - 5. Citations from this work will hereafter be noted in parentheses in the text.

4. Meyer, p. 242.

5. Ibid., p. 241.

6. Ibid., p. 235.

7. T. W. Higginson, "Intensely Human," *Part of a Man's Life* (Boston, 1905), pp. 127, 136.

8. H. M. Jones, "Introduction," *Army Life in a Black Regiment*, pp. xvi - xvii.

9. Meyer, pp. 244 - 45.

Chapter Four

1. *Letters and Journals* . . ., p. 348.

2. T. W. Higginson, *Common Sense About Women* (Boston, 1900), p. 3. Citations from this work will hereafter be noted in parentheses in the text.

3. *Letters and Journals* . . ., p. 279.

Chapter Five

1. T. W. Higginson, *Cheerful Yesterdays*, p. 107.

2. Mary T. Higginson, pp. 278 - 79.

3. Ibid., p. 280.

4. T. W. Higginson, *Malbone: An Oldport Romance*, in *Studies in Romance* (Boston, 1900), p. vii. Citations from this work will hereafter be noted in parentheses in the text.

5. Edelstein, p. 316.

6. Mary T. Higginson, p. 281.

7. Quoted in Edelstein, pp. 314 - 15.

8. T. W. Higginson, "Discontinuance of the Guide-Board," *Book and Heart* (New York, 1899), pp. 3, 12, 6, 11, 9 - 10.

9. Mary T. Higginson, p. 281.

10. T. W. Higginson, *Oldport Days*, in *Studies in Romance*, p. 282. Citations from this work will hereafter be noted in parentheses in the text.

11. Ibid., pp. 157 - 58.

12. *Studies in Romance*, p. 341.

13. Mary T. Higginson, p. 270.

14. T. W. Higginson, "The Monarch of Dreams," in *Studies in Romance*, p. iii. Citations from this work will hereafter be noted in parentheses in the text.

15. *Letters and Journals* . . ., pp. 335 - 36; M. T. Higginson, pp. 311 - 12.

16. T. W. Higginson, *Cheerful Yesterdays*, pp. 326 - 27.

17. H. M. Jones, "Introduction," *Army Life in a Black Regiment*, p. x.

18. T. W. Higginson, *Cheerful Yesterdays*, p. 327.

19. Ibid., p. 328.

20. Ibid., p. 331.

21. Ibid., pp. 357 - 58. See also Higginson's *Hints on Writing and Speech-making* (New York, 1898).

Chapter Six

1. Ralph Waldo Emerson, "History," *Emerson's Essays*, ed. Irwin Edman (New York, 1961), pp. 28, 30.

2. Mary T. Higginson, p. 285.

3. Ibid., pp. 285, 288.

4. Thomas Wentworth Higginson, *Young Folks' History of the United States* (Boston, 1875), p. iii. Citations from this text will hereafter be given in parentheses in the text.

5. J. S. Bassett, "Later Historians," *Cambridge History of American Literature*, ed. W. P. Trent et al. (New York, 1921), III, p. 178.

6. T. W. Higginson, "Preface," *Larger History of the United States* (New York, 1898), p. v. Citations from this text will hereafter be given in parentheses in the text.

7. Edelstein, p. 337.

8. Ibid.

9. T. W. Higginson, *A Book of American Explorers* (Boston, 1877), pp. 5, v.

10. T. W. Higginson, *Travellers and Outlaws: Episodes in American History* (Boston, 1889), p. 89.

11. T. W. Higginson, *English History for American Readers* (New York, 1893), pp. vi, 313.

12. Review of *English History for American Readers*, *Nation*, 57 (1893), 215.

13. Quoted in Edelstein, p. 339.

14. Ibid.

15. Hintz, pp. 2 - 3.

Chapter Seven

1. T. W. Higginson, *Margaret Fuller Ossoli* (Boston, 1890), p. 2. Citations from this work will hereafter be noted in parentheses in the text.

2. T. W. Higginson, *Henry Wadsworth Longfellow* (Boston, 1902), p. 258. Citations from this work will hereafter be noted in parentheses in the text.

3. T. W. Higginson, *John Greenleaf Whittier* (New York, 1902), pp. 1 - 2. Citations from this work will hereafter be noted in parentheses in the text.

4. Mary T. Higginson, p. 263.

5. T. W. Higginson, *Harvard Memorial Biographies* (Cambridge, Mass., 1866), I, pp. iv - v.

6. T. W. Higginson, *Life of Francis Higginson* (New York, 1890), p. 2. Citations from this work will hereafter be noted in parentheses in the text.

7. For a full record of the family, see Higginson's privately printed *Descendants of the Reverend Francis Higginson* (Boston, 1910).

8. T. W. Higginson, *Life and Times of Stephen Higginson* (Boston, 1907), pp. 271 - 72. Citations from this work will hereafter be noted in parentheses in the text.

9. T. W. Higginson, "Note," *Contemporaries* (Boston, 1900), [n.p.]. Citations from this work will hereafter be noted in parentheses in the text.

10. Th. Bentzon (Marie Therese [de Solms] Blanc), *A Typical American: Thomas Wentworth Higginson*, trans. E. M. Waller (London, 1902), p. 67.

Chapter Eight

1. T. W. Higginson, "An Old Latin Text-Book," *Studies in History and Letters* (Boston, 1900), p. 215.

2. For example, "A Charge with Prince Rupert," "Mademoiselle's Campaigns," and "The Puritan Minister."

3. T. W. Higginson, *Studies in History and Letters*, p. 316. Citations from this work will hereafter be given in parentheses in the text.

4. Henry James, *Hawthorne* (New York, 1966), pp. 47, 43 - 44.

5. William Dean Howells, "James's *Hawthorne*," *Atlantic Monthly*, 45 (1880), pp. 282 - 85.

6. *The Letters of Henry James*, ed. Percy Lubbock (New York, 1920), I, pp. 71 - 74.

7. James W. Tuttleton, *The Novel of Manners in America* (Chapel Hill, 1972), pp. 1 - 27.

8. T. W. Higginson, "Tyler's American Literature," *Nation*, 28 (1879), pp. 16 - 17.

9. T. W. Higginson, *A Reader's History of American Literature* (Boston, 1903), pp. 12, 23, 63.

10. Anon., "Thomas Wentworth Higginson," *The Outlook*, 76 (February 6, 1904), p. 338.

160   THOMAS WENTWORTH HIGGINSON

11. T. W. Higginson, *A Reader's History* . . ., p. 168.
12. *Letters and Journals* . . ., pp. 105 - 106.
13. T. W. Higginson, "Ralph Waldo Emerson," *Contemporaries*, p. 5. Citations from this work will hereafter be given in parentheses in the text.
14. T. W. Higginson, "Thoreau," *Short Studies of American Authors* (New York, 1906), pp. 27, 29.
15. T. W. Higginson, "James Russell Lowell," *Nation*, 53 (August 13, 1891), pp. 116 - 118.
16. Ibid.
17. T. W. Higginson, "Lowell," *Old Cambridge* (New York, 1900), pp. 185, 187.
18. T. W. Higginson, *A Reader's History* . . ., p. 159.
19. T. W. Higginson, *Short Studies* . . ., pp. 16, 20.
20. Ibid., pp. 6, 11.
21. T. W. Higginson, *A Reader's History* . . ., p. 91.
22. T. W. Higginson, "Walt Whitman," *Contemporaries*, p. 75. Citations from this work will hereafter be given in parentheses in the text.
23. T. W. Higginson, "Local Fiction," *Book and Heart*, pp. 61, 64.
24. T. W. Higginson, *A Reader's History* . . ., pp. 247 - 248.
25. Ibid., p. 53.
26. T. W. Higginson, *Short Studies* . . ., p. 53.
27. T. W. Higginson, *A Reader's History* . . ., pp. 57 - 58.
28. T. W. Higginson, "Howells's *Undiscovered Country*," *Scribner's*, 20 (1880), p. 795.
29. T. W. Higginson, *Short Studies* . . ., p. 36.
30. T. W. Higginson, *A Reader's History* . . ., p. 255.
31. T. W. Higginson, "A Bit of War Photography," *Book and Heart*, pp. 41 - 43.
32. R. W. B. Lewis, *Edith Wharton: A Biography* (New York, 1975), p. 152.
33. T. W. Higginson, "A Letter to a Young Contributor," *Atlantic*, 9 (1862); reprinted in *Hints on Writing and Speech-making* pp. 19, 29, 38, 40.
34. T. W. Higginson, "Emily Dickinson's Letters," *Atlantic*, 68 (1891); reprinted in *Jubilee: One Hundred Years of the Atlantic*, ed. Edward Weeks and Emily Flint (Boston, 1957), pp. 184 - 85.
35. Ibid., p. 186.
36. Ibid., p. 188.
37. Ibid., p. 193.
38. Ibid., p. 196.
39. Wells, *Dear Preceptor*, p. 209.
40. Quoted in Edelstein, p. 346.
41. Ibid., p. 350.

Chapter Nine

1. Hintz, p. 4.
2. T. W. Higginson, "April Days," *Outdoor Studies and Poems* (Boston, 1900), p. 73.
3. Hintz, p. 8; Pattee (New York, 1915), p. 144.
4. T. W. Higginson, *Cheerful Yesterdays*, p. 1.
5. Ibid., p. 2.
6. H. M. Jones, "Introduction," *Army Life in a Black Regiment*, p. vii.
7. T. W. Higginson, *Cheerful Yesterdays*, p. 363.
8. Ibid., pp. 363 - 64.

Selected Bibliography

PRIMARY SOURCES

For a full list of Higginson's more than five hundred titles, the reader may consult Winifred Mather's *A Bibliography of Thomas Wentworth Higginson* (Cambridge, Mass., 1906) and Mary Thacher Higginson's *Thomas Wentworth Higginson* (Boston: Houghton Mifflin, 1914), as well as footnote references to unlisted items in Tilden G. Edelstein's *Strange Enthusiasm: A Life of Thomas Wentworth Higginson* (New Haven: Yale University Press, 1968). The following is a list, arranged chronologically, of Higginson's major books, editions, and translations.

Thalatta: A Book for the Seaside. Edited by Thomas Wentworth Higginson and Samuel Longfellow. Boston: Ticknor, Reed & Fields, 1853.

Out-door Papers. Boston: Ticknor & Fields, 1863.

Harvard Memorial Biographies. Ed. Thomas Wentworth Higginson. 2 vols. Cambridge, Mass.: Sever & Francis, 1866.

The Works of Epictetus. Trans. Thomas Wentworth Higginson. Boston: Little, Brown, 1866.

Malbone: An Oldport Romance. Boston: Fields, Osgood & Co., 1869.

Army Life in a Black Regiment. Boston: Fields, Osgood & Co., 1870.

Atlantic Essays. Boston: J. R. Osgood & Co., 1871.

Oldport Days. Boston: J. R. Osgood & Co., 1873.

English Statesmen. New York: G. P. Putnam's Sons, 1875.

Young Folks' History of the United States. Boston: Lee and Shepard, 1875.

A Book of American Explorers. Boston: Lee and Shepard, 1877.

Short Studies of American Authors. Boston: Lee and Shepard, 1880.

Common Sense About Women. Boston: Lee and Shepard, 1882.

Margaret Fuller Ossoli. Boston: Houghton Mifflin, 1884.

A Larger History of the United States. New York: Harper, 1885.

Hints on Writing and Speech-making. Boston: Lee and Shepard, 1887.

The Monarch of Dreams. Boston: Lee and Shepard, 1887.

Women and Men. New York: Harper and Brothers, 1888.

The Afternoon Landscape: Poems and Translations. New York: Longmans, Green & Co., 1889.

Travellers and Outlaws. Boston: Lee and Shepard, 1889.

Life of Francis Higginson. New York: Dodd, Mead & Co., 1890.

Poems of Emily Dickinson. Edited by Thomas Wentworth Higginson and Mabel Loomis Todd. Boston: Roberts Brothers, 1890.

Poems of Emily Dickinson: Second Series. Edited by Thomas Wentworth Higginson and Mabel Loomis Todd. Boston: Roberts Brothers, 1891.

Concerning All of Us. New York: Harper & Brothers, 1892.

The New World and the New Book. Boston: Lee and Shepard, 1892.

Such As They Are: Poems. With Mary T. Higginson. Boston: Roberts Brothers, 1893.

English History for American Readers. With Edward Channing. New York: Longmans, Green & Co., 1893.

Massachusetts in the Army and Navy during the Civil War. Edited by Thomas Wentworth Higginson. 2 vols. Boston: Wright & Potter [State Printers], 1895-1896.

Book and Heart: Essays on Literature and Life. New York: Harper & Brothers, 1897.

The Procession of Flowers and Kindred Papers. New York: Longmans, Green & Co., 1897.

Cheerful Yesterdays. Boston: Houghton Mifflin, 1898.

Contemporaries. Boston: Houghton Mifflin, 1899.

The Writings of Thomas Wentworth Higginson. 7 vols. Boston: Houghton Mifflin, 1900. (This edition includes *Cheerful Yesterdays, Contemporaries, Army Life in a Black Regiment, Women and the Alphabet, Studies in Romance, Outdoor Studies: And Poems,* and *Studies in History and Letters.*)

Henry Wadsworth Longfellow. Boston: Houghton Mifflin, 1902.

John Greenleaf Whittier. New York: The Macmillan Co., 1902.

A Reader's History of American Literature. With Henry W. Boynton. Boston: Houghton Mifflin, 1903.

History of the United States. With William MacDonald. New York: Harper & Brothers, 1905.

Part of a Man's Life. Boston: Houghton Mifflin, 1905.

Life and Times of Stephen Higginson. Boston: Houghton Mifflin, 1907.

Things Worth While. New York: B. W. Huebsch, 1908.

Carlyle's Laugh, and Other Surprises. Boston: Houghton Mifflin, 1909.

Descendants of the Reverend Francis Higginson. Boston: Privately Printed, 1910.

SECONDARY SOURCES

1. Book-length Studies

BENTZON, TH. (MARIE THÉRÈSE [DE SOLMS] BLANC) *A Typical American: Thomas Wentworth Higginson.* Trans. E. M. Waller. London: Howard Bell, 1902. The first book-length study, by a French admirer. Full of eccentric opinion, such as the view that Higginson was a "typical" American.

EDELSTEIN, TILDEN G. *Strange Enthusiasm: A Life of Thomas Wentworth Higginson.* New Haven: Yale University Press, 1968. The best study of

Higginson in relation to the social and political history of his time. Indispensable.

HIGGINSON, MARY THACHER. *Thomas Wentworth Higginson: The Story of His Life*. Boston: Houghton Mifflin, 1914. By Higginson's second wife, this family biography presents a valuable though idealized portrait of the man. Indispensable.

HIGGINSON, MARY THACHER, ed. *Letters and Journals of Thomas Wentworth Higginson, 1846-1906*. Boston: Houghton Mifflin, 1921. Indispensable, but containing only a fraction of Higginson's voluminous private papers.

MEYER, HOWARD N. *Colonel of the Black Regiment: The Life of Thomas Wentworth Higginson*. New York: W. W. Norton & Co., 1967. A lively and readable biography for the general reader.

WELLS, ANNA MARY. *Dear Preceptor: The Life and Times of Thomas Wentworth Higginson*. Boston: Houghton Mifflin, 1963. A major study of the man, with special emphasis on his relationship to Emily Dickinson. Indispensable.

2. Dissertations

BRENNAN, SISTER THOMAS CATHERINE, O.P. "Thomas Wentworth Higginson: Reformer and Man of Letters." Michigan State University, 1959. Thoughtful general study.

CROWSON, E. T. "Thomas Wentworth Higginson and the *Atlantic Monthly*." University of Minnesota, 1969. A useful account of Higginson's extensive authorship in our first national magazine.

HINTZ, HOWARD W. "Thomas Wentworth Higginson: Disciple of the 'Newness.' " New York University, 1937. A generously full summary of the writer's whole production.

3. Essays, Articles, Pamphlets, and Chapter Treatments

BLODGETT, GEOFFREY T. "The Mind of the Boston Mugwump," *Mississippi Valley Historical Review*, 48 (1962), 614-34. On Higginson's postwar political position.

BROOKS, VAN WYCK. "The Twilight of New England," *Sketches in Criticism*. New York: E. P. Dutton & Co., 1932. A brief, perceptive account of Higginson by one of our best literary historians.

CAMERON, K. W. "Higginson on Poetry," *Emerson Society Quarterly*, No. 29 (1962), 40 - 42. Brief note on Higginson's poetic criticism.

CHANNING, EDWARD. *Thomas Wentworth Higginson*. Boston: Proceedings of the Massachusetts Historical Society, 1914. A minor appreciation by a co-worker on the histories.

FROTHINGHAM, OCTAVIUS BROOKS. *Transcendentalism in New England*. New York: G. P. Putnam's sons, 1876. Scattered comment on Higginson by the first historian of Transcendentalism, a classmate.

HINTZ, HOWARD W. *Thomas Wentworth Higginson: Disciple of the Newness*. New York: Graduate School of New York University, 1939. A brief pamphlet summarizing Hintz's dissertation, listed above.

HUTCHINSON, WILLIAM R. *The Transcendentalist Ministers: Church Reform in New England*. New Haven: Yale University Press, 1959. A major study of the religious milieu of young Higginson.

JOHNSON, THOMAS H. *Emily Dickinson: An Interpretive Biography*. Cambridge: Harvard University Press, 1955. A severely critical view of Higginson's treatment of the poet.

JONES, HOWARD MUMFORD. "Introduction," *Army Life in a Black Regiment*, by T. W. Higginson. East Lansing: Michigan State University Press, 1960. A brief but discerning appreciation of a "masterpiece."

KATZ, JOSEPH. "The 'Preceptor' and Another Poet: Thomas Wentworth Higginson and Stephen Crane," *Serif*, 5 (1968), 17 - 21. On Higginson and Crane's verse.

McCORMICK, E. L. "Higginson, Emerson, and a National Literature," *Emerson Society Quarterly*, No. 37 (1964), 71 - 73. Emerson's influence on Higginson's Americanism on literature.

McCORMICK, E. L. "Thomas Wentworth Higginson, Poetry Critic for the *Nation*, 1877 - 1903," *Serif*, 2 (1965), 14 - 19. A review of Higginson's poetry criticism in this periodical.

McCORMICK, E. L. "Thoreau and Higginson," *Emerson Society Quarterly*, No. 31 (1963), 75 - 79. A summary of Higginson's view of Thoreau.

QUARLES, BENJAMIN. *The Negro in the Civil War*. Boston: Little, Brown, 1953. Puts into a fuller context the campaigns of the First South Carolina Volunteers.

STANTON, ELIZABETH CADY et al., eds. *History of Woman Suffrage*. 6 vols. New York: Fowler and Wells, &c., 1881 - 1922. A major compendium of suffragist history.

STEVENS, MAUD L. *Colonel Higginson and His Friends in Newport*. Newport: Bulletin of the Newport Historical Society. No. 49. April 1924. An account of the Newport years, which are omitted in *Cheerful Yesterdays*.

WHITE, F. E. "Thomas Wentworth Higginson's Idea of Democracy," *Negro Historical Bulletin*, 6 (1942), 55 - 71. Analyzes Higginson's racial views in relation to the democratic idea.

WILLIAMS, D. H. "Thomas Wentworth Higginson on Thoreau and Maine," *Colby Library Quarterly*, 7 (1965), 29 - 32. On Higginson's appreciation of *The Maine Woods* and other naturalistic prose.

Index

Adams, John 122
Addams, Jane 48
Agassiz, Louis 30
Alcott, Amos Bronson 111, 122, 148
Aldrich, Thomas Bailey 148
American Equal Rights Association 41
Anthony, Susan B. 33, 41, 57
Anti-Imperialist League 47
Anti-Slavery Standard 124
Arnold, Matthew 128
Atlantic Monthly 38, 40, 42 - 43, 55 - 56, 75, 91, 99, 102, 122, 143
Austen, Jane 78, 128

Balzac, Honoré de 133
Bancroft, George 15, 102, 109, 135, 150
Barney, Margaret Dellinger 45
Barney, Wentworth Higginson 45
Bassett, J. S. 104
Bearse, Austin 34
Beecher, Henry Ward 30
Bellamy, Edward 47, 92
Billings, Josh 139
Birney, James G. 123
Blackstone, Sir William 76
Blanc, Thérèse 125
Boston *Evening Transcript* 48
The Boston Quarterly Review 18
Boswell, James 15
Bowditch, Henry 34
Bowditch, Nathaniel 15
Bradstreet, Anne 136
Brook Farm, 22 - 23
Brown, Charles Brockden 136
Brown, John 36 - 38, 122
Browning, Elizabeth Barrett 117
Browning, Robert 15, 91, 135
Brownson, Orestes 17

Bryan, William Jennings 48
Burke, Edmund 120
Burney, Fanny 15, 124
Burns, Anthony 34 - 35, 137
Butler, Benjamin 45
Byron, Lord 15

Cabot, George 119
Caesar 102
Carlyle, Thomas 17, 19
Carnegie, Andrew 47
Century Magazine 122
Channing, Edward 105, 108
Channing, Edward Tyrell 15, 135
Channing, William Ellery 21
Channing, W. F. 35
Channing, William Henry 17, 19, 26, 111
Channing, Mary. See Mary C. Higginson
Child, Lydia Maria 59, 124
Cicero 54
Clarke, James Freeman 17, 23, 27, 111
Coleridge, Samuel Taylor 136
Collins, William 15
Columbus, Christopher 108
Constant, Benjamin 21
Cooper, James Fenimore 82, 105, 134 - 35
Cousin, Victor 21
Crane, Stephen 142, 149
Crusoe, Robinson 108
Cummins, Maria 86
Curtiss, Burrill 19
Curtiss, George 19

Dana, Charles 22
Dana, Richard Henry 14, 35

Darwin, Charles 54, 126, 136
Davis, George T. 111
Declaration of Independence 77, 128
De Forrest, John W. 128
De Soto, Hernando 108
Devons, Charles 33
Dewey, John 48
The Dial 17, 19, 112, 135, 137
Dickinson, Emily 117, 143 - 47, 149
Douglass, Frederick 29, 46
DuBois, W. E. B. 48, 72

Edelstein, Tilden G. 46, 47, 85, 105, 109
Edgeworth, Maria 15
Edwards, Jonathan 134, 136
Ellery, William 108
Emancipation Proclamation 39
Emerson, George B. 44, 103
Emerson, Ralph Waldo 17, 18, 19, 22,
    23, 30, 31, 38, 59, 74, 86, 102, 111,
    122, 126, 129, 135, 138, 139, 148;
    Works Cited: "The American
    Scholar," 17, 115; "The Divinity
    School Address," 17, 136; *Essays*,
    128; "Historic Notes on Life and
    Letters in New England," 17;
    "Literary Ethics," 136; "Man
    Thinking," 36; *Nature*, 17, 74, 91,
    136; "Self-Reliance," 17
Epictetus 17, 41
Essex County Anti-Slavery Society 29
The Estray 20
Examiner and London Review 86

Fichte, Johann Gottlieb 17
Fifty-first Massachusetts Regiment 39
First Religious Society of Newburyport
    26 - 27
First South Carolina Volunteers 39, 49 -
    50, 59 - 73, 114
Foster, Abby 33
Francis, Convers 24
Franklin, Benjamin 134, 136
Free Church of Worcester 33
Free Soil Party 29, 32
Free State Rally 25

Freedman's Aid Society 40
Freeman, Mary Wilkins 140
Freneau, Philip 136
Freud, Sigmund 98
Frothingham, Octavius B. 22
Fugitive Slave Law 32, 36
Fuller, Margaret 14, 17, 19, 83, 122, 133,
    138, 148, 150. Works about:
    *Memoirs of Margaret Fuller;
    Margaret Fuller (Marchesa Ossoli)*
    111.

Gannett, Ezra Styles 24
Garland, Hamlin 87, 141
Garrison, William Lloyd 19, 26, 33, 38,
    43, 107, 123 - 24, 148
Genteel Tradition 92, 148
Gibbon, Edward 102
Goethe, Johann Wolfgang von 102, 113,
    149
Goldsmith, Oliver 15
Grant, Ulysses S. 128
Greeley, Horace 33, 112
Green, A. G. 111
Grimké, Sarah 59, 123

Hale, Edward Everett 26, 46
Haraden, Jonathan 108
The Harbinger 18
Harris, Thaddeus Wiliam 124
Harper's Bazaar 46
Harper's Ferry 37
Harte, Bret 141
Hawthorne, Nathaniel 22, 42, 82, 86,
    105, 139. Works cited: *The
    Blithedale Romance*, 112; "Ethan
    Brand", 98; *The House of the Seven
    Gables*, 119; *The Marble Faun*, 137;
    The Scarlet Letter, 128; "Twice-told
    Tales," 127.
Hawthorne, Sophia 124
Hedge, Frederick H. 111
Hegel, Georg Wilhelm Friedrich 17, 136
Herodotus 102
Hesiod 22
Higginson, Francis 13, 30, 118 - 19

Higginson, John 119

Higginson, Louisa Storrow 13

Higginson, Louisa 44

Higginson, Margaret Waldo 44

Higginson, Mary Channing 21, 27, 35, 38, 41, 87

Higginson, Mary Thatcher 43, 44

Higginson, Stephen 106, 119 - 22

Higginson, Stephen Jr. 13

Higginson, Thomas Wentworth. Birth and education, 13 - 16; experience of transcendentalism, 16 - 19; search for a vocation, 19 - 25; radical ministry at Newburyport, 27 - 30; abolitionism, 30 - 38; Anthony Burns affair, 34 - 36; in Kansas, 36 - 37; ally of John Brown, 37 - 38; Civil War experience, 38 - 39; women's liberation, 40 - 41; literary and political writings, 41 - 48; last years, 49 - 50.

WORKS CITED:

Afternoon Landscape, The 92

"Amos Bronson Alcott" 137

Army Life in a Black Regiment 39, 42, 59 - 73, 83

"An Artist's Creation" 94 - 95

Atlantic Essays 16, 127

Book and Heart: Essays on Literature and Life 49, 87, 133

A Book of American Explorers 53, 107 - 08

Carlyle's Laugh, and Other Surprises 49, 133 - 34

Cheerful Yesterdays 58, 134, 151 - 52

"The Clergy and Reform" 26

Common Sense About Women 45, 74 - 81

Concerning All of Us 133

Contemporaries 133, 135

"Denmark Vesey" 38

English History for American Readers 43, 108

English Statesmen 43

"Gymnastics" 56

"Haitian Emigration" 38

Harvard Memorial Biographies 42, 117 - 18

"The Health of Our Girls" 56

Henry Wadsworth Longfellow 49, 114 - 15

Hints on Writing and Speech-making 45, 99

History of the United States 107

John Greenleaf Whittier 49, 115 - 17

A Larger History of the United States 45, 105 - 107

"Letter to a Young Contributor" 143

"Letters from Kansas" 36

Life and Times of Stephen Higginson 119 - 22

Life of Francis Higginson 45, 118 - 19

Margaret Fuller Ossoli 45, 111 - 14

Malbone: An Oldport Romance 42, 82 - 88, 149

Massachusetts in the Army and Navy during the Civil War 109

"Massachusetts in Mourning" 36

"The Monarch of Dreams" 95 - 99, 149

"My Creed" 52, 54

"Nat Turner's Insurrection" 38

The New World and the New Book 133

"The Next Great Question" 41

Old Cambridge 138

Oldport Days 42, 88 - 91, 93 - 99

Out-door Papers 91

"Ordeal by Battle" 38

Part of a Man's Life 72, 133

"Philanthropy" 52 - 53

"Physical Training" 56

"Ralph Waldo Emerson" 135 - 37

A Reader's History of American Literature 43, 133 - 34, 141

"Saints and Their Bodies" 54 - 56

Short Studies of American Authors 45, 133

Such As They Are: Poems 92

"The Sympathy of Religions" 52, 57

"To Thine Eternal Arms . . ." 50

Travelers and Outlaws 45, 108

"Waiting for the Bugle" 50

"The Woman Who Most Influenced Me" 14
Young Folks' History of the United States 43, 44, 103 - 105
Hintz, Howard W. 110, 148
Hoar, Elizabeth 112
Hoar, Serman 119
Holmes, Abiel 104
Holmes, John 124
Holmes, Oliver Wendell 14, 30, 124, 126, 138, 148, 149
Homer, 22, 104
Howe, Samuel Gridley 34, 37, 43, 59, 124
Howells, William Dean 36, 43, 48, 82, 87, 128, 132 - 33, 141 - 42, 159
Hurlbert, William 82
Huxley, Thomas Henry 54, 126

The Independent 41
Irving, Washington, 14, 82, 135

Jackson, Andrew 105 - 107
Jackson, Helen Hunt 40, 92, 122, 145, 149
James, Henry 82, 87, 128, 131 - 33, 141; Works cited: *The Bostonians*, 141; *The Europeans*, 142; *Hawthorne*, 128; "Madame de Mauves," 141; "The Madonna of the Future," 141; *Roderick Hudson*, 128.
James, William 47, 55
Jefferson, Thomas 77, 105 - 106, 120, 121, 122
Jewett, Sarah Orne 140
Johnson, Andrew 40
Johnson, Samuel 15
Johnson, Thomas H. 145
Jones, Howard Mumford 58, 73, 100

Kant, Immanuel 17
Keats, John 15
Kemp, William 34
Kent, James 76
Kingsley, Charles 82

LaFarge, John 40
Lanier, Sidney, 122, 139
"The Latest Form of Infidelity" 18
Leif the Lucky 108
Leroux, Pierre 21
Lewis, Sinclair 133
The Liberator 25, 123
The Liberty Bell 25
The Liberty News 25
Lincoln, Abraham 60, 77, 128
Livermore, Mary 41
Lowell, James Russell 15, 18 - 19, 46, 68, 75, 99, 105, 113, 118, 126, 138, 148, 149
Lowell, John 119
Longfellow, Henry Wadsworth 14 - 15, 20, 44, 113, 116, 122, 126, 129, 133, 137, 138, 150
Longfellow, Samuel 31, 114

Mabie, Hamilton Wright 148
MacDonald, William 107
Madison, James 121
Marshall, John 15
Mason Committee 37 - 38
Massachusetts Bay Colony 13
Massachusetts Disunison Convention 38
Mather, Cotton 118 - 19, 134, 136
May, Samuel 34, 36
Mazzini, Giuseppe 112
Melville, Herman 82
Meyer, Howard N. 28, 69
Mill, John Stuart 136
Miller, Joaquin 141
Motley, John Lothrop 102, 109
Mott, Lucretia

The Nation 45, 86, 122
The Nationalist 47
National Woman Suffrage Association 41
Naturalism 139, 142 - 43
New Englands Plantation 119
Newburyport *Herald* 27
Newton, Isaac 22

Norris, Frank 142
Norton, Andrews 18
Norton, Charles Eliot 99
Novalis 17

Palfrey, J. G. 24
Parker, Theodore 16, 23, 26, 33, 34, 37, 38, 59, 111
Parkman, Francis 102, 109, 150
Parsons, Charles 14
Pattee, Fred L. 149
Peabody, Andrew 24
Peabody, Joseph 108
Peirce, Benjamin 15
Perkins, C. C. 14
Perkins, Stephen Higginson 19
Petrarch 93 - 94
Phillips, Wendell 19, 26, 28, 33, 34, 38, 69, 124, 148
Pitkin, Timothy 104
Plato 17
Plotinus 57
Plutarch 17
Poe, Edgar Allan 138, 149
Porphry 53
Pratt, Rowena 14
Prescott, William Hickling 102, 109
Prescott, Harriet 28, 91, 135
Proclus 57
Proudhon, Pierre Joseph 152

Quincy, Josiah 15 - 16
Quintilian 54

Realism 87 - 88, 128, 139, 141 - 42
Richter, Jean Paul 21, 79
Ripley, George 17, 22

Sanborn, Frank 37
Sand, George 86
Saxton, Rufus 29, 60, 62 - 63
Schelling, Friedrich W. J. 17
Schleiermacher 17, 24
Schurz, Carl 47

Scott, Walter 15, 68, 128
"The Secret Six" 37, 124
Seneca 17
Sewell, Samuel 30, 119
Shakespeare, William 91
Shays, Daniel 108, 120
Shelley, Percy B. 135
Sherman, William Tecumseh 119
Sims affair 32, 34, 36
Sismondi, Jean 22
Smith Gerrit 37
Smith, Sydney 135
Southworth, Mrs. E.D.E.N. 86
Sparks, Jared 15
Spencer, Herbert 136
Spenser, Edmund 15
Staël, Madame de 20, 80
Stanton, Elizabeth Cady 33, 41, 57
Stearns, G. L. 37
Stedman, E. C. 92, 139, 148
Stone, Lucy 30, 33, 41, 46, 57, 59, 79
Storrow, Nancy 13, 31
Story, William Wetmore 15
Stowe, Harriet Beecher 42
Stowell, Martin 34
Sullivan, William 107
Sumner, Charles 30, 43, 64, 124

Tasso, Torquato 15
Taylor, Edward 136
Taylor, Zachary 29
Tennyson, Alfred Lord 15, 20
Thacheray, William Makepeace 133
Thoreau, Henry David 17, 19, 31, 32, 41, 83, 90, 91, 126, 137 - 38, 148 - 49
Thucydides 102
Ticknor, George 14
Transcendental Club 112
Transcendentalism 16, 18, 19, 51, 57, 112, 136, 137, 148
Todd, Mabel Loomis 49, 142, 146
Tufts, Henry 108
Turgenev, Ivan Sergeevich 142
Turner, Nat 108
Twain, Mark 47, 141

172

Tyler, Moses Coit 134
Tyndall, John 126

Very, Jones 15
Vesey, Denmark 108
Vigiliance Committee 34 - 35
Villard, Fanny Garrison 45
Villard, Oswald Garrison 48

Ward, Artemus 139
Washington, Booker T. 72
Washington, George 122
Weiss, John 26

Wells, William 14
Wharton, Edith 133, 143, 149
White, Maria 19
Whitman, Walt 50, 122, 131, 139 - 40, 149
Whittier, John Greenleaf 29, 32, 43, 46, 92, 115 - 17, 122 - 23, 126, 133, 138, 148
Winthrop, Theodore 82
Woman's Journal 46, 74
Woodhull, Victoria 41

Zola, Emile 142

DATE DUE
